B*R*OKEN CHAIN

B*ROKEN* CHAIN

Catholics Uncover the Holocaust's Hidden Legacy
and Discover Their Jewish Roots

Vera Muller-Paisner

PITCHSTONE PUBLISHING
Charlottesville, Virginia 22901

PITCHSTONE PUBLISHING
Charlottesville, Virginia 22901

H 58386535

Library of Congress Cataloging-in-Publication Data

Muller-Paisner, Vera.
  Broken chain : Catholics uncover the Holocaust's hidden legacy and discover their Jewish
roots / Vera Muller-Paisner.-- 1st ed.
      p. cm.
  Includes bibliographical references.
  ISBN-10: 0-9728875-5-5
  ISBN-13: 978-0-9728875-5-7
1. Jews--Poland--Biography. 2. Jewish children in the Holocaust--Poland--Biography. 3.
Christian converts from Judaism--Poland--Biography. 4. Holocaust, Jewish (1939-1945)--
Poland--Influence. 5. Poland--Ethnic relations. 6. Ronald S. Lauder Foundation--Employees.
I. Title.
  DS135.P63A1524 2005
  940.53'18'0922--dc22
                              2005005903

in memory of my parents and Mary Engel,
and for Ron, Seth, and Amanda

Contents

B_ROKEN CHAIN

Introduction

The rabbi of Warsaw, Michael Schudrich, tells the story of his encounters with Madeleine Albright, who learned in 1997 that three of her four grandparents were Jewish. He met her for the first time at a dinner at the presidential palace in Warsaw shortly after this revelation was made public. Michael introduced himself as a rabbi from the United States working in Poland with Poles raised as Catholics who had recently discovered their Jewish roots. Ever the diplomat, Albright did not flinch. They spoke for a few minutes about how people discover.

Six years later, both were at a reception at the Polish Embassy in Washington, DC. Michael approached her, introduced himself as the rabbi of Warsaw, and reminded her that they had met in Poland several years earlier. She said that indeed she remembered the meeting, recalling that they had spoken on a staircase and he had told her that the Jewish community in Poland was coming back to life. Michael said that he did not think that she remembered him particularly, but remembered the story to which he was associated.

Just as the rabbi with stories of "hidden" Jewish roots seemed to have resonance for Madeleine Albright, many other Americans—including other major political figures, such as Wesley Clark and John Kerry—would no doubt have felt a personal connection to his work. Clark, who served as the supreme allied commander of NATO during the Kosovo war, was raised as a Southern Baptist in

Little Rock, Arkansas, and discovered in his twenties that he descends from generations of rabbis from Minsk on his paternal side.[1] Kerry, meanwhile, who is a practicing Catholic, has known for less than two decades that his paternal grandfather was Jewish. He has been quoted as saying: "It is more than interesting. It is a revelation."[2]

Such "hidden" roots, when uncovered, can change a person's orientation to the world. Known feelings of "sameness" in family religion and tradition are confused and fragmented. The process of reintegrating personal identity and self-acceptance is compelling. Perhaps for this reason the Jewish population in Poland climbed from 4,000 in the early 1990s[3] to more than 20,000 in just a few years[4]—figures that are not attributed to immigration.

Stories in the following chapters were compiled from interviews and support groups I held in Warsaw, Poland, for individuals who learned that they were not Gentiles, as they had believed their whole lives, but were, in fact, Jews. Some learned at the deathbed of an elderly family member who may have revealed the family's secret with a request to be buried in a Jewish cemetery; others learned in no less dramatic ways. For most, the first reaction was one of anxiety. This stemmed, in part, from living in a country where anti-Semitism is common, and jobs and livelihoods are at stake. But it also stemmed from the psychological shock of losing one's identity.

Our family's stories and history inform our sense of identity and provide a narrative to hold on to, add on to, and pass on, creating continuity from one generation to the next. Unless burdened by secrets, we know our family's history and can tell the story of how we came to be. Family characteristics of the past and present become familiar to us. We become connected to the way generations have acted and worshiped. Pain interwoven into a legacy memorializes the moment and accentuates the unity of survival. Each family retells its own interpretation of historical reality, philosophy, and religion within the social structure by which it is surrounded. In turn, families are shaped by both internal and external forces and events.

One has to wonder what it must be like to consider oneself as being an "insider," a part of "us," the greater community or society at large, only to discover the secret of being "the other," a hated outsider. Would there be self-hatred? How would one integrate a sense of self? Would exposure to this conflict help to bring about religious tolerance?

Drawing on my work in Poland and my personal history, these are but some of the questions I will explore in this present work. It is with the greatest admiration for those in this situation that these stories are presented. Perhaps what can be learned from their struggle is acceptance of self and others. The world has become a global community. The need for tolerance is great.

Chapters are drawn from interviews and discussions in the support groups I held, in which participants focused on family secrets and their internal and external struggles with their "new" selves. While I have changed the names of those involved and have modified some of their accounts to maintain confidentiality, these stories are real. They are founded in the forces of war and the struggle for survival. They are about buried family truths—hidden from spouses and children—that have broken the chain of legacy and continuity, and they are about the discovery of those truths that have broken the chain of secrets.

1 War, Trauma, and Memory

My family immigrated to the United States in 1955. We had come from Antwerp, Belgium, hoping to find a new life in America. I did not know then that both of my parents had reinvented their lives after the Holocaust. They had each lost a spouse, children, and family during the war. Were it not for their suffering and subsequent marriage to each other, I would never have been born.

I grew up, as did so many people in this country, surrounded by secrets. They hovered around me in foreign languages. By the time I was five, I was eavesdropping in twice as many languages as I could speak. Spending the first eight years of my life in Belgium, I spoke French in school and Polish with my parents. Secrets always came cloaked in either German or Yiddish within a quiet ritual that demanded attention, even from a child. My memories are of half-said things, the almost palpable feeling of words implied but never uttered, and I have a kind of fascination, even appreciation, for the beauty and power of language on the cusp, language that has not yet been born.

A short time ago, I learned that my family name, Muller, was indeed authentic. I had assumed that it had been created to protect my father from being killed during the Nazi regime. It remained honored and hyphenated along with my married name. Knowing that it is "real" has made me feel less of an impostor. Another piece of my family's

14

identity has been connected, thereby enlarging the clarity of the whole picture.

My sense of identify was defined both by what I knew and thought I knew about my family history. Stories were multilayered, like a finely handmade carpet. Unlike a carpet, however, the stories were not woven in their entirety. I remember stories about my miraculous birth as a first child to a Holocaust survivor who was forty-four. I was not told about her first marriage and the loss of her first husband. Any questions I had about her past led to agitation and dismissal. Fragments of information were difficult to piece together to form a whole history.

Holes in the story of my family represented secrets created by the trauma of war. In the name of protection, lies were told, half-truths uttered. Some fit better than others, but the family's fabric was weaker in those spots, and more vulnerable. Much energy and maintenance was needed to keep the thread of past lies from unraveling. When the fabric fragmented from sudden exposure to secrets, the hole widened and exposed the emptiness of lies. Family tapestries that hide the fabric of lies about collective traumas keep a person from knowing where they come from and who they are. The threads of family legacy become inauthentic.

Family history unfolded for me as I listened to my mother's stories about growing up in Krakow. It was as if we were both girls whispering to each other about what happened the previous summer. The chronology of her life, from her childhood at home with parents and siblings to her present situation with my father and me, was seamless. In these conversations, she would neither mention her first husband nor the interruption of war.

Reshia, my mother, was born in 1903 in Krakow. She lived in Kazimierz, the Jewish quarter, in a large corner house on 36 Krakowska Street, with her parents, one brother, and seven sisters. The family owned two cheese and butter stores, both in Krakow, one being across the street on Krakowska. It was easy for the children to help behind the counter before and after school. Customers watched the family grow as they bought their cheeses. My mother's responsibility when she finished high school was "keeping the books," and sometimes traveling abroad to find special cheeses for the store. She enjoyed working for her father, experiencing him as a warm and loving man. When speaking about her life at home, I slowly became aware that she barely ever mentioned four of her sisters, sisters who I knew on some level had not survived the war. As a child, I was really only aware of having one uncle and three aunts.

After the war, her brother, my uncle David, became a cantor in the biggest synagogue in Vienna. Two of her sisters immigrated to Israel. One was aunt Sara, who was full of life. The other was Aunt Ida, who was the eldest. She was hardly mentioned except when my mother would say in German that she had "the real thing," her way of saying that she was dying of cancer. My mother's favorite sister was aunt Rusia, who lived in Paris and with whom she had experienced countless escapades. Their boldness together while living at home as children ultimately served as practice runs for the boldness needed to survive the war.

I remembered hearing that aunt Rusia had been bold when Jewish families in her town in Czechoslovakia were ordered to pack their bags and proceed to the train station for deportation. Rusia and her husband Sammy left their daughters Lilly and Vera with a trusted maid at her family's farm. Dressed well, they joined this morbid parade of Jewish families and walked separately toward the tracks, without suitcases, before furtively slipping into the line of onlookers on the street. Neither boarded the train.

One of my favorite stories was about the evening my mother and Rusia, still living at home, went to a dance unescorted, a forbidden act for them. They were able to sneak into their bedrooms just before dawn and slip under the bedcovers in evening gowns just before their father checked on all the children before he left for the store. All went well until the oven was lit. Both sisters were morti-fied when a putrid smell whiffed past their nostrils. As it had rained heavily upon their return, they did not want to walk back to their rooms in shoes that were squishy and wet. The pumps that had swirled them around the ballroom in Viennese waltzes and the tango had been hidden in the oven and forgotten. The maid had turned the oven on in preparation for breakfast, causing the house to smell of burning leather. Although both my mother and Rusia were punished, my mother giggled every time she told the story. She spoke in a very animated and easy way about those times.

She spoke about four of her eight siblings as if they lived around the corner and she had seen them the day before. Indeed, the four corresponded weekly. I grew up with my mother reading their let-ters to me during quiet times on Saturdays. When visiting my aunt Rusia in Paris, the same letter reading ritual was performed.

However, when I became curious about the "others," or about the chronology of events, my mother's tone would change, her eyes would glaze, and she would mutter to herself about how a sister was either the most beautiful, the youngest, the favorite, the most tal-ented . . . but that she didn't know, couldn't leave, didn't see what was happening. "What a shame," she would say.

When I asked about specifics, she would avert her eyes and either suddenly become busy with something else or annoyed at my not having done some imaginary task. In later years, I contacted a few of the remaining family members scattered throughout Europe and Israel to help fill the holes in my empty narrative. Most claimed a faulty memory, or ignorance.

My mother was hospitalized suddenly at the age of sixty-nine. I received a call from a cousin who thought it important for me to know that her papers had been falsified and that she was at least ten years older than I was aware. After her death a few weeks later, I learned that she had sworn them all to secrecy to save me from the legacy of trauma.

When I was still young enough only to listen, I fell in love with Krakow. Life sounded wonderful. There were happy summer and winter vacations, sports, the theater, opera, and ballet. My mother was vibrant when she spoke of life before the war. Her hazel eyes widened with glee, while her arms made large gestures as if she were trying to envelope the scope of her beloved medieval city. She spoke of Sabbath meals at her parent's table with a dozen weekly invited guests from the synagogue. The quality of life was high for the thriving Jewish community. Her feelings were filled with powerful emotions. Those moments then and now fill me with powerful emotions as well, but for different reasons. These were the only times that she was available emotionally to me; meeting my gaze and sharing her past happy days. I was able to feel closer to her at these times, a mother who was otherwise difficult to approach and to understand.

These "snapshots" of her past were different in every way to those glimpses I received when I overheard my parents speak in German or Yiddish. They were unaware that I was listening, absorbing their words through all of my senses. There was no levity or laughter; voices were kept low, bodies seemed huddled. I could almost sense the dryness of mouth, could see the clenching of hands and teeth. *I remember the shame of sensing my parents fear and the fear it evoked in me.* This particular behavior was replicated throughout my childhood.

With a childhood that also consisted of laughter-filled vacations and spontaneity, anticipating the mood of the next moment was difficult for me. There were times in my childhood spent only in the company of my father Solomon. A quiet man with interesting hobbies, he played chess with people by mail. There were chessboards in several rooms around our house that were not to be touched. He studied each board and made his changes. I had seen pictures of him dressed in equestrian attire, boots and britches. I could not imagine him on the back of a horse. Even as a child he seemed thin and fragile to me. He explained to me that his health and stamina had been different before the war, but he never went into detail.

There were moments in my childhood when he apologized for my mother's absences, both figuratively and literally. She was totally unavailable at those times and my father came home from work at midday to prepare lunch. I have vague memories of him wrapping slices of chicken with a piece of lettuce and telling me stories while I ate. When we vacationed in Knokke, a summer beach resort in Belgium, I mostly remember spending time with him. He took great care to make unusual and beautiful kites that we would fly on the beach.

On any given day on the beach, children sat in the holes they had dug, displaying handmade papier-mache flowers on a sand shelf they themselves had dug. Other children walked by with their pails, acting as customers. My father was very skilled at creating beautiful flowers for me to sell. I, in turn, was able to purchase other flowers for my collection. The currency exchange was not money. It was a particular little brown shell with a jagged tooth like edge. They were difficult to find and considered very desirable.

I have happy memories of growing up in Europe. I remember neighborhood and school friends. I remember playing in the street in front of our house. It seemed as if everything was close by and easy to walk to. I especially remember my father walking me to school and often coming home for lunch. I was sent to a Yeshiva called Tachkemony. My parents were not religious but wanted me to know "where I came from." It was a far cry from knowing grandparents and being able to feel the rhythm and tradition of a family.

In the winter we would meet aunt Rusia, her husband Sammy, and their two daughters, Lilly and Vera, for ski vacations in Switzerland. My favorite places were Arosa and St. Moritz. I liked Arosa because its sleighs were lined with soft maroon velvet and a toasty warm blanket would be tossed over you as you sat down for the ride. I remember many such rides with my father. I would sit in front and he would sit behind me with his legs on either side of the sled to steer and work the brakes.

St. Moritz was special to me for other reasons. When we took the ski lift, we would pass the clouds and see distant planes at eye level. I also remember looking forward to having "frites" in the outdoor restaurant on top of one of the slopes. Inevitably my mother would put cream on her face and bask in the sun as I ate them. I also enjoyed the walks and seeing horse races on the frozen lake in the winter.

The voyage to America on the *Queen Elizabeth* was pleasant but was a precursor to the tension that would follow. I had a glass menagerie that was too fragile to be sent by freight, so my mother had allowed me to bring it on the ship. I placed the figures on the stand close to my bed. One day the seas turned rough and Bambi, my favorite, fell, shattering a leg. I remember feeling very upset but not being able to get sympathy from either parent regarding my loss. Although it felt important to me at the time, it was the smallest of losses compared to life that followed.

We docked in New York and were driven to a prearranged apartment on 191st Street off St. Nicholas Avenue in Washington Heights. I was to go to school about eight blocks away at the Yeshiva Rabbi Moses Soloveichik. I was grateful that at least the Hebrew would be familiar to me since I did not speak a word of English.

Gone were the days of my father walking me to school or coming home for lunch. When I came home from school, it was inevitably to an empty apartment. My father would give me a job to do until their return. Every day there was a new box of Good & Plenty candy sitting on the window sill for me. I was responsible for cutting each piece of candy into four or five slivers. I felt honored to be trusted with a knife and did my job dutifully. My father usually arrived before I finished the entire box. He would praise my work and remove the candy. I never asked what happened to it or why I needed to cut more the next day. It was my job, and I felt pride doing it.

My father suddenly disappeared from my life when I was about nine. I remember thinking that my world had ended. We had been at my parents' friend's apartment for Sunday brunch, and I remember my father began to feel ill. I was whisked away to a friend's house. My mother told me that my father had been hospitalized and children were not allowed to call or visit the hospital. I'm not sure how long I thought him ill. I remember arguing with a girlfriend who said that she had heard that my father was dead. I insisted that he was in the hospital. I remember her saying that they didn't keep dead people in the hospital. When I told my mother about the argument and asked where my father was, she reiterated that he was in the hospital and would be home soon. She told me not to listen to others. Eventually, when my father did not return, I begged just to hear his voice, and that's when she told me that he had indeed died. *Years later I learned from a cousin that he had died of a heart attack at the friend's house that afternoon.*

The communication between my mother and me was filled with unresolved fragments of information. With my father gone, I was aware, even as a child, that I was not receiving the kind of information needed for daily life. My mother had come to conclusions about past experience and was not always aware or ready to share information needed in the moment. Not only could I not ask, I could not be heard. It was only easy to communicate about happy thoughts and positive feelings.

Fears were unacknowledged. I was often fearful of coming home from school by myself since there was an active gang, headed by a punk known as Billy, roaming my neighborhood. I had told my mother about having been threatened several times, but she refused to listen. When I told her that two boys held me down while a third tried to get me to eat an apple that had been poisoned, she told me that it must have been my imagination. Things like that didn't happen here, she would say. Someone was playing tricks on me. When I was run down by a gang member on a bicycle and shoved against a car, the black and blue marks that I showed her met with a simple response: I needed to be more careful and to move out of the way of approaching bicycles. After many of these incidents, some more dangerous than others, I stopped telling her.

One day, in yet another frightening moment, two gang members surprised me in front of my apartment building, grabbed me, and hoisted me upside down from the fire escape. I was dangling above the entrance, from two stories up, wondering whether this was the time that I would actually be killed. Suddenly everyone scattered! I looked behind me and saw my mother in the distance, coming home. I was incredibly grateful when I saw her and began crying. Surely when she saw me she would realize the stories that I had told her were not exaggerations. I started calling out to her. She looked everywhere but couldn't see me. I told her to look up. Finally, she saw me. When our eyes met I started to try to tell her what happened, but she simply wagged a finger and told me to "get down from there, this instant." She then walked into the building. I felt betrayed. I had thought that she would be able to make my world safer. Clearly, I was mistaken and alone.

A few years later when it was time to go to high school, without consulting my mother I decided to take an entrance exam to a Yeshiva in Manhattan. I was accepted on scholarship, breaking the news to my mother by telling her to dress properly as we were going to meet the principal of my new school. She didn't understand how I had managed to get accepted and only questioned me once about the reason for not going to the local high school. I simply told her that it was dangerous and she never asked me again.

Looking back I realize that it was not possible for her to think that I might be in danger. I suppose she needed to believe that everything dangerous was behind her and Washington Heights was a safe harbor for her young daughter.

In my teens and twenties, I tried to understand my family history more by asking direct questions, yet the stories she told stayed oddly intact, the same, without beginning or end. I asked my mother, for example, how it happened that I was named after my first cousin in Paris, Rusia's daughter Vera, who was living, knowing that in the Jewish religion, one is only named after a dead relative. "You see," she replied, "I was her favorite aunt with whom she had been staying, and I was trying to get her home to her parents in Czechoslovakia, as times were becoming dangerous. I dressed her in her pretty new coat and asked her not to speak Yiddish on the train, since it was full of German soldiers." Nevertheless, my mother continued, Vera started to sing a Yiddish song and the soldiers noticed and ran after them. Jumping off the train, my mother said she embraced little Vera, protecting her from the shots being fired at them. "I told myself that if we both survived and I ever gave birth to a daughter, she would share her name."

My mother told this story and others like it without emotion. If I dared show any emotion as she related these stories, such as fear at being shot, I was treated as if I should have known and understood the situation. I often felt that I had to learn to act like her, so that I too would be able to escape if faced with a similar situation.

Years later when visiting my aunt Rusia in Paris, I asked her about the story of her daughter Vera and my mother on that dangerous train ride. As she started to tell the story, I anticipated hearing about the shots that had just missed killing both my mother and her daughter. As it turned out, I was little prepared for what I heard. Indeed, my mother was my cousin's favorite aunt, with whom she had been visiting in Krakow. When it became apparent that moving to safer quarters was necessary, my uncle Sammy wanted his daughter Vera to be brought back home. Vera was too anxious to travel with the maid and cried for my mother to return with her. My mother complied, leaving her *family*, who would not be able to stay and wait for her return. Just when I felt I knew, I realized there was no complete knowing. I was to find out later that this, too, was only half a truth. Stories were interwoven; there were other secrets, silences, inside the spoken words.

Daily conversation between my mother and me remained superficial: "Where did you go?" "What did you do?" "When did you eat last? Aren't you hungry?" I found myself wondering about superficial questions floating on the surface of underlying trauma. Yet, my mother had a hearty and contagious laugh. It seemed to burst from her in an uncontrollable way. I didn't understand how it was possible for her to separate herself from the pain. Now after years of graduate work in psychology and certification in psychoanalysis, I am just barely able to grasp it intellectually.

As I reworked having been raised by two Holocaust survivors in my own analysis, I learned to understand and integrate the "holes" in my history.[5] To this day, "not knowing" remains more natural to me than "knowing." I can easily help others integrate the "holes" in their own stories, but writing about myself is very difficult. I need to be reminded about what I am not telling.

My reality includes taking precautions and "being prepared." A valid passport is more important to me than to most people I know. I am also deeply afraid of anti-Semitism. The scud missile attacks against Israel during the Gulf War affected me strongly. Although I was thousands of miles away, my thoughts immediately turned to gas masks and fears of being gassed. *I wondered if I would have survived the war, and wondered what my parents had done to survive.*

As Holocaust survivors living in Israel needed to "hide" in a "safe room" and confront past traumas with the use of gas masks, I was grateful that my mother's death in 1982 saved her from being a witness to such cruel reminders of past events. Aunt Rusia in Paris was not spared, however.

When I called to speak to her the day after one attack on Israel, her thought process and wording had regressed. She stammered and kept repeating the same sentence. She lived alone in a large apartment in Paris on one of the main boulevards and found herself living in the part of the apartment furthest away from the front windows. As she walked from room to room she locked the door behind her. This level of distress was highly unusual for her. I spent a long time talking with her and called her several times a day for the next few days until her mindset improved. When my aunt called me a few days later, sounding calmer and more like "herself," I started to think about the ease with which old traumas revisit and reshape the reality of the current sense of self.

I wondered how many others were struggling alone, with holes in their identity related to the Holocaust or other traumas, condemned to ruminate among fragments of their life's narrative.

Once in private practice, although trauma was familiar to me, I did not initially focus on the transmission of war-related traumas in families. Suddenly, this seemed like a grave omission. I had somehow not considered tapping the reservoir of my personal experiences for use in my professional life. *Another connection to identity unfolded.*

2 Secrets Unearthed

When not working with patients, I became immersed in the available literature on survivors of war-related traumas and the long-term effects of trauma on family. Going to conferences and listening to experts in the field of trauma led me to want to be involved in the process of supporting the families of survivors, beginning with families of Holocaust survivors. Yael Danieli, a leading clinician and researcher in the field of trauma, was kind enough to share her ideas with me and answer my questions.

In 1989, I decided to start a local support group, as a community service, for children of Holocaust survivors in Stamford, Connecticut, the town in which I live. I approached several Jewish agencies in the area. Most said that they didn't think there was a need for such a group. Finally, Ben Greenspan, the director of Jewish Family Services in Stamford, offered to give the idea some thought. He invited me to the organization's next board of directors meeting. He was not sure what the board, several of whom were Holocaust survivors, would think about a support group for children of Holocaust survivors, but he agreed to put it on the agenda.

At the meeting, I was asked to defend the need for the group. I said studies have shown that psychological reverberations of traumatic events can affect other family members, producing profound implications for subsequent generations. Effects may be overt with symptoms manifesting as emotional disturbance or may be very subtle in which the child of a survivor identifies with the trauma. The board members listened with interest but weren't sure that it applied to their community.

Although I hadn't planned on it, I told them the following story: In the middle of the night in the dead of winter many years ago, a heavy snow had covered our house like a blanket. My children were small and sleeping in their rooms; my husband and I were asleep in ours. In an instant, my husband and I bolted upright, awakened by a loud noise, which sounded like an explosion. Being aroused from a sound sleep, my first instinct was to take the children, grab cash, and escape. My U.S.-born husband told me to remain calm while he went downstairs to see what had caused the blast. He thought it was probably the boiler—not an air raid. Although I have never heard the sounds of war, I realized I shared some of the same fears and vague nightmares about it as survivors.

I told them my vision for the group was for members to become aware of, share, and be able to help each other integrate pieces of transmitted trauma in order to inhibit its effects on succeeding generations. The board saw the potential value of the support group and voted to offer it to the community on a trial basis. Press releases led a dozen people to the first meeting.

The question that went around the room most often after initial introductions was, "Where was your family before the war?" *It reminded me of "papers please." It was as if everyone in the room had two identities.* Men and women, mostly working professionals, were leaving behind their current life and identity, going back to a time before they were born, to family life before or during World War II.

The weekly meetings at Jewish Family Services, although held in Connecticut, led immediately to prior Eastern European addresses and times. The calendar turned back to the 1940s. Descriptions of towns and family status came first. "My father's factory employed one hundred workers in Lvov. Imagine that!" said Peter, a doctor. Again and again members tried to understand and to help each other reconstruct the missing pieces. There was an urgency to the discussions. They talked about the whereabouts and degree of suffering of their families during the war. Family history and trauma seemed more vital and close to the surface than current family life.

Blanca, an artist, recalled that her mother once spoke about the Germans beating her near a submarine. She thought it happened in Switzerland but was unable to understand the story. Her mother never talked further about it; now her father was dead and her mother was senile and unavailable. She related another story about her parents running from Spain and the brutality of Francisco Franco. Steven, another member, was able to tell her what he knew. He said that he remembered reading about a work camp near the foot of the Pyrenees where submarines for the Germans were made. That additional piece of information was a good lead and very helpful. Blanca thanked him.

The telling of family stories was often prefaced with apologies for a bad memory. It was difficult to remember sequences, dates, and names of camps, cities, and ghettos. Everyone soon realized that they were not alone and that their memories were not at fault. Many parents who were willing to discuss endured traumas did not have the capacity to weave and develop the narrative within a historical framework.[6] Their stories hung like prints strung on a line in the darkroom, waiting to be developed, each representing just one chapter of their family history.

In the first support group, Stella, whose family escaped by hiding in woods and barns, remembered feeling envious of friends in the United States who had plastic-covered family picture albums that included pictures of at least one or two generations of family. It was as if the stories had themselves become picture albums to these children of survivors.

The lack of sameness to those who had family albums on the coffee table was recognized by most as a factor that set them apart and made assimilation more difficult for them. There was both envy and pain in the room, as each member recollected the scanty and torn remnants of family photos that had survived the war. Each photo was precious, as was each painfully told story.

The transmission of these traumatic memories was accompanied by a world view of life being both random and precarious. There was a sense of unreality in the attempt to bear witness to a past family trauma, an event the present group members had no personal memory of. Everyone wondered whether they would have been able to make life-saving decisions during the war. One needed to be vigilant to be able to escape.

I watched people as they sat with the silence in the room. It was a different silence because you knew it was the silence that sits at the edge of speech, as opposed to the silence that smothers speech. *Listening to the silence—and the stories—brought me back, again and again, to memories of my own childhood. When I was eighteen I had discovered pictures of my mother with a man other than my father in the back of aunt Rusia's closet in Paris. That is how I found out that my mother had been married before the war, and that her husband had been shot trying to come back and get her out of the ghetto. She had made the choice to leave her husband to take Vera back to Czechoslovakia. More secrets inside the seemingly spoken words.*

During the next few years groups continued. New members were accepted after every eight-week cycle. Many participants elected to stay for several months, some for a year or more.

During this time, at conferences for survivors of the Holocaust, I elected to have groups available for spouses of Holocaust survivors, spouses who had not suffered directly from the Holocaust. These groups were very popular and were called "Living with a Survivor." Adults, as well as children living in the house with a survivor, were grateful to talk to others. I remember one spouse, Barry, who had been a pilot during the war and had flown fifty missions over oil fields to destroy fuel reserves for German aircraft. I remember hearing how dangerous those missions had been, with many American pilots and crews dying in the attempt. Barry had protected his wife, who had suffered in a concentration camp and had lost most of her family, from knowing the details and traumas of his flights. He felt that his trauma could not compare with hers, although there were times when he would have liked to talk to her about it. Most spouses felt a need to protect the survivor from any more suffering and to be strong for them.

At one of these conferences I met Dori Laub, a professor of psychiatry at the Yale University School of Medicine, who was also conducting a group. We talked about our mutual interest regarding the study of trauma. Soon after this meeting he founded the International Study Group for Trauma, Violence and Genocide at Yale University. His vision was for various disciplines at universities around the world to coordinate their studies of trauma. For two years I worked as a research consultant for Dr. Laub and helped to coordinate an international retreat. I will always be grateful for his vision, which gave me the opportunity to absorb various points of view about trauma.

As my groups were ongoing, I sometimes interviewed prospective members who felt uncomfortable about joining because they had been raised Christian only to discover in adulthood that they had hidden Jewish roots. Over a ten-year period about ten percent of group members fell in this category. Some of their parents had converted, some had "made believe" being Christian, and others had avoided religious commitment. Each discovery was surprising and, generally, had not been volunteered by the parent.

Robert, for example, discovered Jewish family roots when he was fifty. He had called a distant family member in England for information regarding the family tree. He was told that his family had moved to England to escape Nazi persecution. On further investigation, he discovered that it was for being Jewish. "I was raised as an Episcopalian and attended church every week with my mother," he said. "Jewish roots never occurred to me. In fact, I don't remember knowing anyone Jewish in England."

Christian said that he didn't know about Jewish roots until a few years ago when he was in his thirties:

I was raised in Europe as a Catholic and remembered my mother making negative comments about Jews. I heard similar comments at school, so I didn't think too much about it, and felt lucky that I was not a member of that "tribe." I also remembered that my father remained silent during these moments. On a trip back home to see my parents as an adult, I was struck by the same pattern in my parents' behavior. I asked my father why mother hated Jews so much and also why he remained so silent.

My father was not able to respond at the moment but the next day he took me to an old Jewish cemetery and pointed to his mother's grave. He had married a Christian, but his family was Jewish. Life became much more difficult for him and my mother during the war. His religion had put them both at risk and he was not able to work openly. He told me that he stole potatoes and sometimes eggs from the local farmers. She stayed with him, but the hardships they endured had created resentments.

Growing up I remember my father working very long hours and not being home with us much. I guess that was his way of making things up to my mother. Knowing helped me to understand the bitterness in the household. I experienced a quiet anger but could not grasp it.

Lisa, a young woman, told how she traveled across the country to see her grandmother. She had always loved her grandmother and was looking forward to introducing her to the man she planned to marry, a Jew. She said she knew that her grandmother would be supportive although her mother had not been. She then related the following:

> It pained my grandmother to see me in such conflict. During our visit, grandmother removed a shoebox from the closet in a ceremonial way and produced a fading yellow-cloth Jewish star, while telling us the story of her life in Europe, during the war. I was both shocked and elated to learn that she was Jewish but simultaneously furious with my mother. When I called mother to tell her what I had learned, she became enraged. She felt betrayed and exposed by the secret being told and tried to convince me that it would be safer for our Jewish roots to remain a secret! I told her that she was in America now and didn't need to fear being a Jew. She said that there was no safety in being a Jew anywhere.

There were many variations on the effects of living with family secrets. In one case, twin sisters had survived the war, each feeling differently about their identity as Jews. One sister left for the United States as soon as possible while the other remained in Poland. Both married, had children, and settled down to daily life. Anna, the twin in the United States, maintained the family's Jewish tradition, while Mala, the twin in Poland, kept her Jewish roots secret, married a Catholic man, and led a Christian life.

The sisters saw each other once yearly, when Anna would visit Poland. Upon each visit Mala was fearful that the secret of her Jewish roots would be exposed. Anna understood, kept her twin's past Jewish roots a secret, and would even accompany her to church. Although uncomfortable with the charade, all went well for the sisters until one of Mala's children had been accepted to an American university within driving distance from Anna. It was a wonderful opportunity for the daughter but caused great stress for the twins. Mala begged her sister to remove all religious Jewish items from her home when her daughter came to visit. It was naive to think that would be a solution as the family led an open Jewish life. Anna would not hear of such an intrusion into her life.

The entire group simply suggested that she tell her niece that she had married a Jew and converted. This suggestion immediately unleashed feelings that had remained dormant for many years. Anna said angrily, "This solution is giving in to Hitler. I am proud to be a Jew and would not consider hiding my identity the way my sister did. Although I love my sister, I will not allow myself to be victimized by her fears!"

When first joining the group, members considered these secrets as part of the past and one of the travails of life that needed to be controlled and hidden. Each felt alone, not realizing that this moment in history had given birth to legacies that would one day cause strangers to come together. It was becoming more obvious that these secrets had profoundly affected lives and were very much in the present. Both knowing and not knowing created conflicts. What role, if any, had not knowing and discovering the secrets of religious identity played in their life cycle?

I found myself wondering whether it was coincidental that some of those who discovered the secret in the years close to courtship had not married, and of the ones who had, many did not have children.

For the first time in my professional life I felt as though I was using myself fully. I wanted to learn more about the conflict of being raised as a Christian and discovering a secret Jewish heritage.

A split occurs when parents convert from one religion to another after a profound trauma, such as the Holocaust, particularly when they keep their conversion secret from their children. Upon discovering the family secret, confusion about identity arises; this conflict continues to be carried through various life-cycle events, such as marriage and the rearing of children.[7] Should I marry a Christian or a Jew? should my child go to church or to temple?

In normal development, identification with parents and important adults feeds the evolving sense of self. Feelings of well-being and intimacy surround these identifications, including the experience of a family's religion. Knowing and feeling the "sameness" in one's family, only to discover that one has been living with a false identity, creates a family that may no longer share the same values or religion. Families may become split, with children feeling that they have to choose one parent or religion over the other. I wondered how I could learn more about reconciliation after the discovery of secret Jewish identity disclosure.

It occurred to me to speak to people who had been born Jewish yet raised Catholic. Having conducted workshops years earlier for a conference of "Hidden Children" in Canada, I called one of the organizers and explained my dilemma. She referred me to a woman who had recently spent time in Poland, a Holocaust survivor who had been in search of personal family archives. I was told that individuals were discovering their roots at the deathbeds of parents or grandparents, who would say that they were Jews and ask to be buried in Jewish cemeteries. I wondered, why wait until their last breaths? Why share the secret at all?

During Poland's traumatic Communist post–World War II years, as well as during the 1968 nationwide purge of Jews, many children of Holocaust survivors who remained in Poland chose to conceal their Jewish roots. Like their own parents after the Holocaust, they often concealed their background from their spouses and their children. In a Catholic country where church and state were united, prayers and religion were taught in school. Therefore, all children were raised Catholic by default.

The year 1989 reflected the end of communism and the beginning of this search for roots. At the beginning of 1990 there were approximately 4,000 Jews in Poland. Within five years there were between 10,000 and 20,000. This trend continued steadily without immigration into Poland adding to the numbers.

I discovered that the Ronald S. Lauder Foundation had been in Warsaw since 1988 helping those who wanted to explore their Jewish roots through educational programs and other activities. Further, I learned that the foundation sponsored an archivist to help with the search for Jewish roots and a rabbi to help in the exploration of religious identity. There was little if any information regarding Judaism in Poland and fewer prayer books. With this newfound freedom to explore, the timing was right. Freedom, however, would not be able to control the inner turbulence created by the unfolding of discovered secrets. I wanted to learn the process that integration demands, but would I allow myself to go to Poland? Most of my parent's families had never left Poland alive. How could I go?

Both of my parents had died, secrets intact, leaving a large hole in my own history. I knew I wanted to answer some pointed professional questions, but I also knew that I would have personal issues to confront. The trip would be as much an immersion into my own psyche as it would be an exploration of the psychosocial phenomena of integrating a secret in one's identity.

I used my professional identity as a shield against my own personal vulnerability and wrote a letter to the Lauder Foundation. Enclosing a pertinent resume, I asked for an introduction to the rabbi involved in its Jewish-roots project in Warsaw. I did not think that interviews would be possible without the support of a trusted leader.

The foundation responded generously with the name of the rabbi, his phone number, and a note stating that he would be expecting to hear from me. I also received an e-mail from the archivist of the Ronald S. Lauder Genealogy Project at the Jewish Historical Institute of Poland. He explained the critical role the foundation served in helping individuals find members of their family so long after the war. He outlined his work in detail and added the contact name of a Jewish community leader in Poland.

My first phone call was to Rabbi Michael Schudrich. After several conversations over a short period of time, he suggested that if interviews were to be conducted at all, they would be best suited at Rychwald, a "camp" in the Polish countryside created by the Lauder Foundation for those interested in learning more about Judaism. People came alone, he said, or with their families for a few weeks at a time. Rabbi Schudrich suggested I consider coming for two weeks. He thought it would be important for people to have time to get to know me and to feel relaxed about being interviewed. I respected his wishes and was professionally comfortable with the idea.

I remember how unsettled I felt about going. I didn't realize then how much I needed to experience the feel and scent of Poland firsthand.

3 Learning the Ropes

The plane was packed with people speaking Polish. I somehow expected to know them and have them recognize me as my mother's daughter. During the flight I felt myself passing figuratively through time and space. There was a primitive, personal shift in me. I both yearned to be the daughter and struggled to be the adult and professional. As the plane touched down on Polish soil, I felt a combination of excitement and guilt, as if I were being unfaithful to the memory of my parents. I wondered whether they would have approved of this trip. My gut feeling was that my father would have been supportive and my mother would have been against my ever entering Poland. Escaping from three work camps to come home to Krakow was difficult enough. It was wrenching for my mother to discover how little of her family had survived.

One day, she had told me once, she was walking aimlessly down the street when she bumped into a woman who had worked in her family's home for many years. She was pleased to see a familiar face. The woman, however, was not happy to see her. She said, "I see they didn't kill you, why did you come back?" My mother was stunned. She looked her straight in the eye and noticed that the woman was wearing her favorite hat! My mother felt betrayed. Poles were not friends to Jews and were not to be trusted. As I stepped off the ramp, I thought of my parents and, with tears in my eyes, walked toward the arrival area.

The airport's arrival area was like many others in the world. There were a certain number of booths through which all who entered the country pass to display their passports and other documentation. Lines formed as flights arrived, the volume and rhythm of passport stampings ever increasing. I found myself thinking about Jews hoping to escape during the war by passing borders with falsified papers, papers that did not identify them as Jewish. Of course my U.S. passport did not specify my religion, but the primitive part of me wanted to turn and run before I was "found out."

Someone was to meet me at the airport and take me to the offices of the Ronald S. Lauder Foundation[8] where I would wait several hours before boarding a train. As I came through the customs door, anxious and wheeling my bag, a tall older man with a shock of white hair caught my attention. He was holding up a sign with my name on it. I felt relieved and approached him. He seemed surprised that I spoke Polish and explained that he was to drive me to the train station from where we would head to the Lauder Foundation. We drove through the center of Warsaw where new office buildings mingled with buildings still partially exposed and unprotected—artifacts of the war.

There was a quiet comfort in using Polish again on my arrival in Warsaw. I hadn't spoken a word of it for fifteen years, not since my mother's death. Though I was born in French-speaking Brussels in 1947, Polish was my mother tongue. It was my first time in Poland, yet there was a sense of familiarity. I was to travel by train, four hours south of Warsaw to Bielsko-Biyala, which was one hour's distance from Krakow. I was curious and had looked at a map to see if any towns sounded familiar. I recognized the names of places that I had heard about in my childhood. Stories of wonder and excitement were always prefaced with the phrase "before the war," as if Poland had not survived. I'm not sure if I expected Poland to be intact. In fact, the countryside was lovely. I found myself trying to see it through my mother's eyes, in its innocence, before the slaughter and burial of millions of Jews.

The train station had the sing-song loudspeaker quality of many modern European train stations, but with its own strong stench of urine and unsavory characters. I was told to be wary, to hold on to my belongings, and to spend as little time as possible on the platform. Thefts at knife point were common both on the platform and on the train. I was advised to pay the conductor a small fee and shown how to make that transaction, in order to be seated in the "safest" wagon for the journey. I was grateful to be shown "the ropes."

Finally, we arrived at the Ronald S. Lauder Foundation to find it nearly empty. The staff was at a summer camp. A policeman stood guard outside while a caretaker couple was in the office to assist those who came in with questions or problems. Several people came in having trouble finding apartments and kosher food; an old man came in requesting a hearing aid. People came in constantly during my three-hour stay. Some had concrete problems; others were in search of Jewish relatives. I asked how many hours a day the office was open.

The matronly female caretaker looked at me for a long moment, smiled, and explained slowly as if speaking to a child that they were open for as long as people needed them. At times Jews came in at night and needed a place to stay. Being the caretaker and living in an apartment on the property made it possible for her to help them. The caretakers were an elderly couple that had weathered Poland's turbulent times and were happy to be involved in its struggle to grow. Panni Marisha (a formal diminutive), as she was called by all, stood erect in her petite frame, giving the appearance of a much taller person. She wore her hair tightly clasped in a salt and pepper bun, which accentuated her long neck and added to the severity of her face. The man who had met me at the airport, her husband, appeared to be an extension of her appearance for he was very tall and thin. He was the "handyman" and was capable of taking care of the building, just as she was capable of helping all who entered it. We spoke about anti-Semitism and I asked her why she chose to stay in Poland. She said that Poland's soil was rich with Jewish blood and she felt that leaving would be the same as abandonment, particularly as there was a chance of revitalizing the Jewish community.

Before World War II there were over 3 million Jews in Poland, comprising 9.8 percent of the population.[9] A thriving Jewish community such as existed in prewar Poland had more than just strength in numbers. It was composed of Jewish families unified by Talmudic precepts. Jewish communities helped to conduct Jewish life by supporting religious functionaries, synagogues, and ritual baths, providing religious instruction for the young and supplies of kosher meat, watching over community assets, supervising welfare institutions, and maintaining cemeteries. The 1921 census allowed Jews to claim their religion as a nationality, which created an official split between being Jewish and being Polish.

My thoughts returned to the several phone conversations I had had with Michael Schudrich, the American rabbi who had been working for the Lauder Foundation for six years, trying to help rebuild the Jewish community in Poland. He was my contact, my way in, so people would dare to speak to me. How would I talk to these people? How could I break, so to speak, the ice? *I thought of ice, of cold camp winters, of black-branched trees against a landscape so white that it seared.* I wasn't sure people would want me to enter that world with them, a place very private and dangerous. I had accepted his suggestion that I come to a summer camp, a two-week session in which I would mingle with people of the second and third generation, people who had either hidden being Jewish or had just discovered their heritage.

It was dusk as the train pulled into the station. It slowly exhausted its last breath of steam as my heart began to race. Most passengers had left the platform. A lone young male, wearing a black leather jacket and an earring, stood arms folded against the fender of a car. His name was Jacek and he had been sent as my driver. On the hour trip to "camp" he spoke of his nostalgia for the times of martial law when he was able to spend more time with friends and working in the black market had been a challenge. Leaving Poland now, he said, was impossible, as visas were hard to get and the outside world "didn't want Poles" any more than the Poles in Poland wanted Jews.

We finally arrived at camp Rychwald, situated in the middle of the south Polish countryside. As the car pulled up, I heard songs often sung after dinner in Jewish homes. The swastika on the wall outside the camp was shocking, but no more than hearing Hebrew melodies in the middle of Poland. I felt both proud and scared. It was a beautiful setting. There were three large Spanish-style buildings on several acres of enclosed property, with an inviting large iron gate at the entrance, closed only at night. Following the sound of melodious voices I found myself at a large dining hall. The room was filled with about one hundred youngsters singing while stomping hands on the table in rhythm. Leading them with great enthusiasm was Rabbi Schudrich, a strong, athletic man in his forties with dark eyes and beard. With a loosened tie and rolled up sleeves, he was clapping, singing, and moving between the aisles of tables. Upon seeing me, he approached to introduce himself, invited me to dine and share in the evening's events, and had someone show me to my room, all while not missing a beat in his movement.

We had earlier discussed the manner in which I would mix with those present in order to make people comfortable about being interviewed, although there had been no guarantees that interviews would be possible. Rabbi Schudrich, or Michael, as everyone called him, including the young, was very protective, and would decide whether interviews would be a good idea, after I had been in camp for several days to a week. Indeed, that first week helped me to understand the questions to ask and gave me the opportunity to listen to the various disruptions that had occurred with the discovery of Jewish roots, particularly in a country where Jews had once been destroyed and at present remained unwelcome.

When casually speaking to people, I never asked about their

backgrounds, yet they often talked about it nevertheless, as if rehearsing their new identity, or practicing saying it out loud in a place that was safe. For example, one evening I met Marianna, a medical doctor who was standing outside of the main house engaged in a heated discussion about the uncertain future of young Jews in Poland. Dark haired and petite, she spoke with passion as she waived her lit cigarette against the evening sky. I was very taken with her fervor, poise, and confidence. How long had she known about her Jewish roots and what effects did it have on her life?

When the discussion was over I introduced myself and started by asking questions about the conversation that I had just heard. Marianna said she had sent her children to study abroad so that they might more freely choose their religious identity. She didn't think that would be possible in Poland. I thought her very courageous to be exploring her Jewish identity knowing the disruption it would cause her family life, and told her so. She said compared to her mother, who had exposed herself to danger to give Marianna life and freedom, her sacrifice for her children's future was much smaller. She then lowered her gaze and started to tell me her story, much of which she herself had only recently learned.

Marianna had been smuggled out of the Warsaw ghetto hidden under her mother's coat when she was four-months old. Her mother had managed to convince a Christian family to take her in and care for her until she could return. She gave them money as compensation for the danger of keeping a Jewish baby. Her mother and father never returned. As the money ran out, she was handed over to other families. She was transferred three times until she was finally placed with a couple who kept her.

Although raised as a Catholic, she remembered being called a "Jew" as a youngster because of her dark complexion. She persevered with her studies and went to medical school. Marianna longed to be part of the community and as a doctor felt needed by it. She married a simple man. He was less educated, worked in the trades, and was very kind. Together, they had two children. As a doctor in a small town, life was good for her until the woman she knew as her mother lay dying. She told Marianna the true story of her adoption. Marianna was "troubled and anguished" by the revelation. Although she was shocked, she said she was somehow not surprised, as she had felt different for most of her life. She tried to learn more more about her history and had spent the previous three summers at Rychwald with her family. Her Christian husband had been supportive and although she continued to work as a doctor in her town, her husband had been denied work because it became known that he was married to a Jew. Although disappointed in her community, she said she was familiar with disappointment and abandonment.

While at Rychwald, I noticed that she was reticent about going to temple and remained on the margin during most events. She was insecure in areas that were so alien to her. As it was the eve of the Sabbath, I wished her a good Sabbath and asked her if she wanted to accompany me to temple. She told me to go ahead and stayed on the sidelines. I entered and sat in the front row where there were many empty seats. I soon learned that people jammed into the back rows. They felt unworthy to sit in the front because they didn't think they knew enough and were not comfortable with what seemed to them like foreign prayers. Within a few minutes Marianna came and sat next to me and whispered apologetically that she knew nothing about Jewish services. I told her that it did not matter and thanked her for coming. I handed her a Polish prayer book that had been transcribed phonetically and in a few minutes I heard her voice in song. I found myself in tears. I wondered if, being in her shoes, I would have had her courage.

I spent the next several days helping team leaders with their programs, which included hunts for Jewish-related objects, staged plays teaching about the lives of famous Jewish leaders, and other educational games and workshops. All programs were informal and voluntary and were meant to help teach Jewish history, life, and religion to those who wanted to know but were afraid to ask.

The camp's assistant director was a Pole whose father was Jewish. He had converted to Judaism in his mid-thirties. It was a difficult and strenuous undertaking for him and included circumcision and rigorous study. Most people felt very comfortable with him. He smiled easily and understood people's confusion regarding religion. We worked well together and became friends. I had the utmost respect for his enthusiasm and dedication to helping others explore their Jewish identities. Although he wore a skullcap while at work in camp and in Warsaw, he told me that he removed it when visiting his family in the outskirts of Warsaw to protect them, as anti-Semitism there still ran strong.

Most of the camp's attendees had stories about how they learned they were Jewish, and how they subsequently told friends and coworkers about their discovery, if they did at all. Many parents had waited until they were old and dying to tell their children of their hidden roots, thereby placing them in a very difficult position. Members of this second generation were almost uniformly afraid of loosing their jobs, their relationships, their friends, and their hard-earned status in society, all while being in the midst of a personal identity crisis. They often felt like "nobodies," neither Polish nor Jewish. Further, the consensus of the local Poles and remaining Jews was that they were neither authentic Poles nor Jews. Many wondered what life would be like for their children, the next generation, if they followed their Jewish heritage. Indeed, some members of this second generation chose to keep this secret a secret and told no one of their Jewish roots.

Interestingly, sometimes third generation children, starting in late adolescence, had taken up the cause of investigating their hidden roots. Young people in their late teens and early twenties were attempting to learn about their Jewish heritage. Some parents forbade this exploration or its exposure to other siblings. There were even families where one child had discovered the truth about one parent, who insisted that it be kept a secret from the other parent. Youngsters felt torn and were trying to shore up newly discovered gaps in identity by leaving home, no longer able to tolerate the internal and external split. It would have been important and constructive to better understand all the conflicts and maintain family cohesion under these circumstances. I needed to interview parents and children to better comprehend individual and family dynamics after the discovery of secret identities.

After several days, a curiosity had developed about my presence, and Michael asked me to give a casual presentation about my work in the United States and my interest in the discovery of Jewish identity in Poland, and to answer any questions they might have. Attendance was high. Questions centered mainly around identity issues. Many were curious about Jewish life in the United States, with some expressing disbelief that Jews in the United States were thriving and not subject to the same discrimination and anti-Semitism they experienced in Poland.

The presentation had gone well. Michael told the staff that I would be doing interviews and to let the assistant director know the names of people who seemed to be likely candidates. A protocol for asking about being interviewed was established so as to lessen any feelings of discomfort. Only the name of a person who had agreed to an interview would be given to me and I would then arrange a mutually convenient time. I heard myself speaking at the staff meeting and answering questions as a professional, while also feeling like the daughter of a Holocaust survivor who was about to break a taboo. I was going to ask questions about the war, questions about secrets and murder, questions that I had not been allowed to ask of my own family. I was going to witness and experience their answers and be supportive, in their mother tongue.

4 Agnieszka, Felix, and Marek

Agnieszka was the first name given to me. She was a pretty, fair-haired girl of seventeen, whom I had noticed earlier. Popular with her peers, she filled the air with a wonderful laugh and wore a small gold cross on a chain around her neck, which she habitually moved back and forth between her thumb and index finger.

The interviews were held in a small room with a window facing the back woods. As I sat waiting for her to arrive, I opened the window, as it was a very warm morning, and found myself listening to a bird's melody. I listened to the rhythm and took a deep breath. I wondered if my Polish would be fluid. I was nervous. She arrived on time and seated herself gracefully. I asked her, as I would nineteen others, to start by stating her age, the age when she discovered her Jewish roots, her manner of discovery, and the effect that information had on her life. The interview questions needed to be broad enough so that I would learn what I didn't know to ask. I was speaking in Polish and was surprised when she asked which language to use for the interview. I told her to use a language that felt comfortable to her. She explained that she would use English as she was tired of thinking about it in Polish and wanted the opportunity to see how well she would express herself in another tongue. Nothing was as expected. I wondered whether the use of another language was self-protective. She was fluent in English and paused at times due to the pain she was experiencing and not because of any difficulty with the language.

She had discovered that she was Jewish one year earlier. She paused, saying that the circumstances had been difficult. Her parents were traveling on vacation and she was sent to spend time with her grandmother. While there, her grandmother was involved in a fatal car accident and died before getting to a hospital. Not being able to reach her parents immediately and feeling panic, Agnieszka called her aunt in a neighboring country. Her aunt came immediately to help with funeral arrangements.

Agnieszka was puzzled by the surname on the death certificate, which sounded Jewish. She asked her aunt about it and was told that indeed the surname was Jewish and that she and her mother were Jewish. Further, her aunt told her this is something neither her father nor her brother knows. As she was trying to digest this shocking information—and her grandmother's sudden death—her aunt told her that this secret must remain with her. However, Agnieszka loved her father and brother and didn't want to keep this secret from them, saying she would speak to her mother about this matter as soon as possible.

"I asked my aunt," Agnieszka said, "how she found out." She was told that her grandmother had never revealed the secret to anyone but her husband. Years earlier, when her aunt became suspicious after she found a letter and confronted her, she finally admitted to being Jewish. Agnieszka's mother was then told but had to vow never to divulge the family secret. Her aunt wouldn't pledge to keep the secret, living outside of Poland, but Agnieszka's mother had not told anyone.

I asked Agnieszka how this secret affected her religious identity. Holding onto her cross with her face tightened, she said, "I am Catholic, well . . . now I don't know what to think about it. In a low voice she added, "I'm lost." Agnieszka had asked her aunt to take the time to tell her the little family history that she knew. She was told that her grandmother survived the war by hiding under garden tools in a small shed on the Aryan side of her town. She foraged for food only at night, weather permitting. Hearing this, Agnieszka felt more connected to her grandmother than ever before and wished that she had known earlier so that she could have asked questions and understood more about what life had been like during a war where Jews were hiding for their lives. We talked about her grandmother's survival and the continuation of her family line. If her grandmother had perished, neither her mother nor she would have been born. *Conversely, if both of my parent's spouses had survived, I would not have been born.*

Agnieszka wanted to know more of the truth. She asked her mother whether or not they were Jewish. Her mother denied it saying that the name on the death certificate was false. She said that people often changed their names during those times. Agnieszka remained persistent until her mother acquiesced and told her the truth, making her promise not to tell her father or brother. This added additional strain on the household, as there were times when she had heard unpleasant things said about Jews in her home. Additionally, she heard anti-Semitic remarks in the Catholic school she attended and often had to stop from saying anything that would draw attention to herself. She mentioned that certain students were known to make comments like "Jewish people to the gas" and to draw a Star of David at the end of a hangman's noose. If dissatisfied with the results of a soccer game, others would write the name of the losing team within the borders of a Star of David. She said such graffiti was common on neighborhood walls. Jewish symbols were used in other instances as well to represent disgust and distaste with something.

It seemed to me that Agnieszka was bursting with this secret and didn't like the burden of keeping it from her father and brother. I asked her what holding onto this secret was like for her. She said that it had changed her relationship with her family. She felt angry and betrayed by her mother for not being trusted enough to be told. She really couldn't understand why her mother continued to keep her Jewish roots hidden from her husband. She understood that the family had made fun of Jews, but surely her father would understand. I asked her what she was going to do. Although she was not planning to expose the secret, it had already caused her harm, as she felt distant from both her father and brother, even though she knew they had done nothing wrong. It was she who had changed, simply by becoming aware of the secret of her heritage. She felt that she was being unfair to her family and to both the broader Catholic and Jewish congregations. She remained in between the two, not knowing whether she was going to remain a practicing Catholic or become Jewish in an ethnic way. The only certainty she had was her allegiance and identity as a Pole.

We spoke about her sense of alienation from her family and her feeling alone in the world although external conditions remained the same. The secret had disconnected her from her life. I could do no more than sit with her and listen to her pain. If she told her father, her mother would be exposed and furious. I wondered if time would help to solve this dilemma or to soften the pain.

Nineteen-year-old Felix stood in between these two worlds as well, but in a slightly different fashion. Tall and slim, he was a young man on his own, living alone while finishing school. He walked with a swagger, as if to music, moving his head from left to right, as he viewed the world through his vibrant blue eyes. He often spent time sitting on the grass under the shade of a tree while waiting for his turn at table tennis. He smiled a lot and usually had a cigarette in one hand. Indeed, I found him as he was watching a game of table tennis. I sat down next to him and said hello. He smiled.

He told me that his parents had divorced and were living in separate cities. Neither seemed available to him. His grandmother, who had died the summer before, had left him a small sum of money with which he was trying to finish his studies. He was on his own and wasn't sure whether studying in Poland would offer him the best future. We talked about this being an important moment in his life in terms of direction. There were various possibilities and directions. I could see that he needed and wanted a mentor. There were so many complications regarding discovery that couldn't be predicted. He wanted to know about university life in the United States. I was careful not to be too enthusiastic about opportunities, as I understood that it was difficult to get a visa to the United States and didn't want to discuss possibilities that would not be available to him. I asked him whether he had ever discussed his future with Michael. He responded by saying that Michael was very busy with matters more urgent than his. I asked him whether he would like me to speak to Michael regarding his future. He beamed and thanked me in advance.

I asked Felix how he found out that he was Jewish. He said that he started to suspect that he had Jewish roots when he discovered a few years earlier that his grandmother, although a practicing Catholic, was quietly attending new programs available for Jews. When he asked his family about this, they told him to stop dwelling on it, as they were all Catholic. He then asked his grandmother directly and she told him that she had been born Jewish and had lived in Germany before the war. During the war she was able to pass as a Catholic, her blond hair and blue eyes saving her from being killed or being sent to a concentration camp. Following the war, she continued the deception, married a Catholic, and lived in Warsaw. Before Felix was able to ask her for more information, she died.

His parents, separated and living in different cities, were preoccupied with their new lives, leaving him to commute between them both. It seemed to him that his grandmother had cared more about him than had his parents. He remembered her listening to cassettes of Jewish music with a smile on her face. Hearing the same melodies at the camp reminded him of her. Building on the love of music she had instilled in him, he eventually learned to dance and was talented enough to win ballroom competitions. Discovery had enriched a life, he said, that had been otherwise empty and sterile.

He looked forward to learning more about his family's heritage and becoming more connected to his family's roots.

He felt awkward, however, when attending synagogue. Jewish teenagers from the United States prayed easily and knew how to act in synagogue, he said. "They know so much more than me. They have been Jews their entire lifetime." He spent evenings reading Polish translations to better understand the prayers. When I asked whether he would like to say more about his life or family, he said that he didn't usually like to say even this much. Nevertheless, during the following weeks when we saw each other across the courtyard, he often approached and asked whether he could walk me to the next building. We talked about his thoughts and impressions. I found him to be very courageous, as were most of the other young people there.

I wondered if youth, in particular, allowed for this sense of idealism about having Jewish roots. Most adolescents appeared less afraid at this stage of life than those whose discovery occurred at a later age. They had brought their guitars and board games. Their music and laughter—the sounds of normal adolescent fun—could be heard late into the night. It seemed that they were able to put aside their identity crises, or deal with them through their music and adolescent group sharing. Some approached me wanting to know about teenage life in the United States. It became obvious to them that life as a teenager and Jew in America was easier. I was often told about the problems at home regarding assimilation. However, optimism was more prevalent in their age group than in the older groups. This seemed encouraging for the future.

Marek told me his story with aired disbelief. A few years earlier, he had decided to change his surname to an earlier name held by his family, as this was common among his friends. He investigated previous family names and discovered that his grandparents, who had both died before he was ten, had been Jewish. As far as he had known, his family had always been practicing Catholics, including those grandparents, who had attended church every week. Shocked, he confronted his parents, who denied the truth for several years. By the time he was twenty-four, he had worn his parents down enough that they finally told him the truth. He was certain that he wanted to learn about Jewish traditions but felt uncertain about his religious future. He was not in a current relationship with a woman and had not thought about how he would want to raise his future children.

As we discussed this issue he wondered aloud whether his not being in a relationship was due to his sense of confusion, as he had always been social and had been at ease with girlfriends in the past. A very good-looking virile young man, he had only just realized that following his Jewish roots would present difficulties in finding an eligible marriage partner. As a non-Jewish girl in Poland would not likely marry a Jew, he would have to look for a mate in Poland's small Jewish community. Life seemed more complex and complicated than he had imagined. He smiled and shook his head at what seemed to be an impossible and paralyzing decision. Should he remain a Catholic or follow his Jewish roots?

Ula had come to a similar conclusion when her mother told her that she had Jewish roots. Her first response was one of horror and devastation. She didn't think that she would be able to consider marriage until she sorted out her religious identity and wasn't sure to whom she would be considered acceptable. At twenty-three, she already felt as though her biological clock was ticking. She felt that time was working against her and wished she had "known" earlier to have more time in which to integrate the information.

The age at which the discovery was made tended to bring with it specific anxieties. Adolescents worried their classmates would treat them differently at school. Young adults worried this would affect their chances at marriage. Older adults feared that their spouse would respond negatively and that it would affect their employability. Indeed, the older one was at discovery, the more potent and troublesome it seemed. When children were involved, decisions about whether or not to tell them and at what age also needed to be considered. This was especially significant given religious instruction continued to be part of many school curriculums in Poland. Children who did not go to religious classes were thought to be Jews or Gypsies and often treated as outcasts. Further, discovering that one was a member of a tribe that was traditionally disliked by the family itself was particularly difficult to digest. Ambivalence about wanting to know was often coupled with wanting to be known and accepted.

Alex had been told by his mother that he was Jewish only six months before coming to Rychwald. I asked him if he knew why his mother decided to tell him then and whether he had had earlier suspicions. He said his mother decided to tell him only after she had discovered there were places for Jews to meet and learn about Jewish traditions. Only seventeen, he felt completely overwhelmed. He had gone to church his entire life, and all of his friends in school were Catholic. Additionally, all of his grandparents had been buried in Catholic cemeteries, even his mother's parents.

In school he had always gone to religion class and would need to decide whether or not to drop out. He mentioned that there was a girl in his school who was the only one who didn't go to "religion." He knew this created problems for her. She was called names and was isolated from her classmates. He seemed anxious and afraid. Indeed, shortly after he arrived at Rychwald he experienced anti-Semitism firsthand. He told me that he and his new friends had gone for a walk one evening and were a few hundred feet past the front gate when skinheads approached them looking for a fight. He said there was a great intolerance for Jews in Poland and needed to spend time deciding his future. He added that his mother hoped he would attend Jewish programs at the Lauder Foundation and regularly go to synagogue.

Although far from his town, he had gone to synagogue several times and was interested in meeting other Jewish youths. He told me that a bubble had burst around the life that he knew and loved so well. One day life was balanced and simple, with a "sameness" in his school, in his church, and in his friendships. The next day, he had lost his "safe" spot and became part of a largely untolerated minority. Although he expressed a willingness to explore his Jewish history, he said this was only because it was important to his mother. He would have preferred not to be burdened with this legacy.

For some, the loss was felt over time. Rysia, a seventeen-year-old girl, had learned that her father was Jewish when she was fourteen. She intercepted a package from Israel that had arrived for him. Although admitting to being Jewish and having family members in Israel, her father did not think it advisable to tell her any more. She lived in a small town and had often heard anti-Semitic jokes in school, although she had never met a Jew and didn't know anyone else who had. Her father had given her a map of Israel with permission to hang it on her bedroom wall, with the understanding that she would not discuss it outside of the house.

One day boys with whom she had been in grade school started calling her a "Jew who should be thrown to the gas." She stood her ground and asked why they had changed, as she hadn't. They told her that they had heard from others that she had "Jewish banners" in her room, which were visible from the street when her light was on. She explained that they had all been friends when they were younger and expected to be treated like an old friend rather than an enemy. Though they never again treated her as a friend, they did not continue to behave aggressively toward her.

Janus, a young man of eighteen, told me a painful story that he said would end with a twist. He had had a best friend for many years but was afraid to tell him that he had discovered his Jewish roots. The secret was difficult for him to withhold, especially as he was sure that it would not make a difference in the friendship. On a day like many others, his friend came to his house to study and noticed a skullcap on the floor near the dining room table. When he asked what it was, Janus said he didn't know and that it may have been dropped by one of his parent's friends. The next day in school, everyone, including the boy who had been his "best friend," ignored him. He couldn't believe it and was very upset at the loss of his friend. Although the two never regained their friendship, Janus said he smiled when he learned, two years later, that his anti-Semitic friend had learned about his own Jewish roots!

There were even accounts of families in which two generations discovered their Jewish roots simultaneously. For example, sixteen-year-old Magda and her mother discovered their Jewish roots at the same time. The mother's brother had died suddenly, and his widow called to invite them both to the funeral, which was in a Jewish cemetery. The grieving widow told mother and daughter what she knew about their family. She gave them details about the where-abouts of the mother's parents during the war, and how they had survived. Whereas they had told the son about their past, they had withheld the information from Magda's mother to "protect" her. Both mother and daughter were in shock. Magda did not know what she would do. She continued going to church, but was antici-pating problems: she didn't know whom to tell or whom to marry, and didn't know how she'd raise her children. The anxieties of her mother, meanwhile, were centered on the future of her marriage and the welfare of her children.

Piotr was nineteen and had never felt close to any religion. He had attended religion class in school only to avoid embarrassment and problems with his classmates. When he was twelve he had seen his grandfather pray in a way unknown to him. He asked his moth-er about this and was told that his grandfather was Jewish. Piotr felt that living among Catholics in a Catholic land should have made it easy for him to choose a Catholic life. Lately, however, he had found himself exploring his Jewish side, yet he didn't feel as if he truly belonged in the Jewish community. "Whoever is Jewish directly from the mother's side is considered more authentically Jewish," he noted. "It's not as desirable from a father's side, so that makes me even farther away from being a Jew."

His grandfather's funeral at a Jewish cemetery impacted him greatly. He wanted to know more about his heritage and discovered that his grandfather had many brothers, three of whom had left Poland before the war, including one who had left for Israel. His grandfather had elected to stay in Poland with his wife and child, who one day while he was out were snatched by the Germans from their apartment. While trying to find them, he himself was taken captive in Warsaw. He soon escaped but never heard from his wife or child again. Piotr felt connected to his grandfather's story. His attempt to more fully understand his family's past, he believed, would help him in his search for life's religious meaning.

5 Double Lives

The response of teenagers to questions of hidden Jewish roots reflects an immediacy of the moment. The urge to discover one's identity exists regardless of parental pressure and surrounding conditions. Conflicts become more complicated with age. Adults think more about family history, their place in society, and their parental responsibilities. With older individuals, therefore, responses to my questions were often not as direct. Many felt the need to first describe the climate of the times.

For example, when I asked Tomasz how old he was when he discovered that he was Jewish, he smiled and said that it was a very good question. Rather than answering my question, he recalled that his interest in Judaism started in the mid-1980s when books about Jews and their connection to Poland's history became available in the country. "You know," he said, "there were periods of time when information about Jewish culture became more available . . . There was always a strong attraction to learn about Jewish life in Eastern Europe. I remember times when you couldn't find a book on the market about it."

He told me that the first real access he had to published material about Judaism was at the beginning of Solidarity in 1980. He said that the second break was in 1989 and has continued ever since. He said that the collapse of communism had just as much influence on people's lives as it did on the economy, affecting several levels of society. With freedom of speech and the freedom to establish organizations came a changed societal system. "There was a period of two years when all old limits were broken," he noted. "It was a revolution in communications. There was the publishing of many kind of books, of behaving in any way, and the first free press. It was at that time that I read books about Polish culture and Yiddish writers like Isaac Singer as well as some descriptions of the process of becoming a Jew."

Tomasz explained that he had been baptized, as had everyone in Poland. He said he was pressed to go to church not so much by family, but by his peers at school. Additionally, his father, born in a traditional peasant family, was happy when he went, so he went from time to time to make him happy, though his mother was indifferent to his churchgoing. I asked him whether he knew of anyone in his family who was Jewish. He answered: "No, not then."

Eventually, he moved to Warsaw, he said, away from his family. Though he observed no religion, in the early 1990s he became interested in mysticism, which was then becoming popular. He started to think about God and His existence. Wanting to know more about possible Jewish roots, which he had long suspected his family had, he made contact with one of his uncles who worked in a historical foundation. Ultimately, he found no Jewish roots on his father's side. Showing great perseverance, he decided to travel to the part of Poland where his grandmother on his mother's side lived. He asked her about the family's history, but she didn't seem to know much and he found nothing unusual in her recollections. Frustrated, Tomasz spent time in the Jewish History Institute in Warsaw looking through unpublished documents. Finally, he found a woman with the same last name as his grandmother. Her address showed that she lived in Germany.

Tomasz wrote her a letter in German asking about the family name and a possible connection to Judaism. He discovered that his grandfather on his mother's side had been in Germany working as a Polish peasant. It showed in the document that he had moved to

Lublin and was then perhaps taken to a local work camp. I asked Tomasz whether he had shared this information with his mother. He said that he had but that she said nothing openly. She told him that it was a "fantasy." When he tried to suggest what had really happened, that his grandfather had been sent to the camp because he was Jewish, she became upset.

He assured his mother that he wanted to stay in Poland, was not going to Israel, and had no ambition to be a rabbi. At the time of this interview the truth was still unknown to him, which created some practical problems. He was engaged to a woman who had found proof that she was Jewish. If he couldn't find Jewish roots, he felt that he would need to convert to Judaism before getting married or having children. "The problem is that when you convert you have to follow certain obligations, and I know that I just couldn't do them," he said. "You can't just be partially converted. I hope that I find some additional information."

He stated he still had some old attitudes regarding religious dogma and he was trying to find a balance, but he was increasingly drawn to Judaism. He told me that he had had a discussion about his search with a friend who offered him advice by using the metaphor of an empty cup. His friend said that it didn't matter that the cup was empty at that moment. Rather, it was only important that it was the same cup, that the form was the same. Tomasz found this concept very interesting. "Religious dogma is for me very much of an empty cup," he said. "I'm a very simple man and need to put something inside, even if the wine is not as great as the old wine." He added that his parents considered this—his turn to Judaism—a radical move and decided to suspend contact with him.

Tomasz began to peek in the windows of the synagogue in Warsaw but found he was afraid to go in. He had heard that there was a conflict between the society of old Jews and the society of so-called new Jews. He said the old Jews were strongly connected with the Cultural Social Association of Jews in Poland and have known one another for over fifty years. "They are uninterested in connecting with new Jews for two reasons," he said. "First, they do not trust outsiders since these minority associations were infiltrated for years by security services, which monitored their conversations and activities. The second reason is that they say that the younger Jews can't understand about being Jewish because they did not endure the hardships."

The first time that he ventured into the synagogue, however, he found Rabbi Schudrich, who was friendly and inspirational: "Here is an American who comes to Poland to teach Polish Jews about tradition. Poland, which in the past had major influence on so many other countries and Jewish communities in the world, has the situation reversed and needs to import an American Rabbi . . . We can say that we are Jews today, but sadly there is a fundamental difference in character and culture between the Jews today and the Jews of our history."

Tomasz asked pensively how the conditions of modern America influenced me as a Jew. "From which direction comes another cup of wine?" he continued. "I'm not speaking about orthodoxy, because with orthodoxy you could live on the moon and it wouldn't make a difference. I'm talking about the edge between the sophisticated modern world and Judaism. Is there a competition?"

I responded by saying that in America it is easy, very easy, to be a Jew. Judaism, or any religion practiced in America, is quite open to interpretation. There are many choices and different levels of Jewish communities. It need not be a competition. I wondered whether his idea of competition came from the inexperience of knowing freedom. "After not being free, the availability of choices must feel overwhelming," I said. "The personal sacrifice needed to take part in a collective religious community is self imposed, not a demand. It is a process that follows a willing heart and from which the cup of wine is filled."

Tomasz wondered how many years it would take to really understand the idea of freedom and thought that freedom and love are two of the most misunderstood ideas. He also wondered whether there was a way to foster the process. He asked me whether I had seen changes in the people of Poland. I told him that I was just beginning to visit the country so it was too soon to tell. He hoped that there would be changes for me to see as the process of democracy grew. We agreed to continue the dialogue when next we saw each other.

At Rychwald, I would often take long walks on the country roads or through the forest. When not alone, I often walked with Jacek in the morning, as the dew rose from the grass. A homeopathic doctor, he was a knowledgeable guide about berries and herbs found growing in the meadows. Jacek was familiar with where things grew and made wild berries appear as if by command. His familiarity with the order of wild roots ran contrary to the disorder and secrecy of his Jewish roots. He walked and talked very fast using great strides as if to compensate for the length of time that it had taken him to learn about his family history. He came to Rychwald to explore his sense of validity as a Christian and Jew and to think about its meaning for his future.

Jacek was thirty-nine when I met him and had been "feeling" Jewish since he was fourteen. It was then that he started being both intellectually and spiritually interested. He started searching for Jewish memorabilia and wanted to study Hasidism. Many things related to Judaism interested him and he wondered why. I asked him if he in fact knew at that time that he was Jewish. He said he thought then that he might be but didn't find out directly until he was thirty-two.

While Jacek was working in Germany, his father had come to visit him. It was the end of communism and his father was more open to talking about the past. Jacek also thought that his father sensed that he did not have much time left. Indeed, he died within a few years of that visit. He said his father started to tell him about his grandfather and great grandfather. "I had asked him why we didn't have any mementos, or any information about his father, yet had so much about my grandmother, including pictures and even identity cards from Germany as well as cards from czarist times."

Whenever Jacek asked him for details, his father would tell him that all of the papers had been burned. When Jacek wanted to go back to where they had lived to do a thorough search for any information, his father told him that he had already done that and there was nothing to be found, everything had been destroyed. His father told him that they had come from Hungary, but Jacek didn't believe it because even if all their mementos had been burnt, there would have been something of Hungarian culture that remained.

Jacek said that the story that his father told him was that his great grandfather was Polish and emigrated to Brazil where he made a fortune. He returned to Poland and bought a large business firm. Jacek was unable to get responses to questions regarding the exact kind of work his great grandfather did, how he made his money, and the kind of firm that he had started. Jacek learned that in the first days of the war, his great grandfather was killed by neighbors. They shot him in the head. I asked why? Jacek suspected it was because he was Jewish.

The story about my grandfather was also strange. He was a sergeant in the army before the war and seemed to have spent most of his time hiding. In 1939 he had fought against the Germans and, from that time on, the Gestapo was looking for him. It seemed to me that the Gestapo did not seek soldiers who were in the regular army. When I asked why, I was told that that's how it was. After the war, my grandfather divorced my grandmother and married twice more. My family had no further communication with him.

Jacek said that these lack of memories have always been with him. His family, he recalled, always seemed different than the families of his friends from school. There were never any anti-Semitic utterances at home, not even common colloquialisms such as "you have a head for business like a Jew" or "you are thrifty like a Jew." He said they didn't go to church and no one ever raised the theme of Judaism or religion. He intuitively knew that it was very unusual for a family in Poland to behave this way. He learned at home that all people were equal.

While Jacek said that he had tried to get closer to Judaism in 1981, he felt unwelcome when he went to synagogue. He thinks that this was because the congregation thought he was a government spy, watching them, so he stopped going. When he returned from Germany in 1992, he went again. This time he felt welcome. By then he also knew for certain that his father was Jewish. His mother had confirmed this after his father's death earlier that year. He later learned out about the Lauder Foundation, met Michael, and started going to synagogue regularly.

I asked Jacek what it was like to be a Jew in Poland. He replied by saying it was a matter of character. "If one is not strong enough to be independent, one can feel as if there are obstacles in every direction," he maintained. "You hear anti-Semitism on television, you feel it in the newspapers, but because I came across it before and in Germany, it does not bother me much."

When asked how it affected his work, he said that he was self-employed and did not hesitate to discuss having Jewish roots with patients if the subject came up. "Somehow most come back," he said. "Some did leave, however, and I know that one patient told others that 'this German doctor is a Jew, don't go back to him. He's involved in dark business deals.'" Jacek found the comment ridiculous and could only laugh at the remarks, as did most of his patients. He said it reminded him of primary school when he was told by a teacher that he had a "Jewish head." I asked what happened. He said he told his mother. A strong woman, she told him that regardless of what others said about him, he was fine just as he was. He said after speaking with his mother he felt good about himself and was no longer affected by such comments.

Jacek said that he felt as though his exploration of Judaism had given him a spiritual grounding. Before, he often felt unattached to everything and everyone, and found that very tiring. Now, he said he enjoyed listening to Yiddish music and reading Jewish stories. He knew that pursuing Judaism more seriously would mean getting circumcised and possibly exposing himself to danger from extremist elements in the community, but he found this empowering. "I suppose that I feel better connected to a commitment with possible danger than to be committed to nothing," he said. "As I talk about it and analyze myself I feel strangely lifted, as if my soul has found its place. I feel awakened and perhaps ready to make a decision that could be dangerous but would put me in a position to protect a belief together with others, and a sense of belonging comes over me. I feel more willing to even give up my life for something meaningful."

He said he finally understood the "Schmah" (Listen oh Israel, our God is one), often the last words a religious Jew will say before death. Further, he said he finally understood the story of the Masada and "how they could have decided on death, even though they could have surrendered." He knew that intellectually what he felt was illogical, because one should care for one's life above all else, but this did not concern him. "You can cross the border into something that doesn't look logical on a materialistic level but has transcended into something more meaningful and spiritual," he noted, "where the soul becomes more important than the flesh."

Jacek was searching for a connection and meaning. I wondered whether his having been called a Jew in his youth had affected him more than he thought. Perhaps it had made him feel alone, different, and caused a schism in his internal world that he was now trying to repair.

6 Identity and Torment for Parent and Child

I listened as people struggled with wanting to both know and not know the secrets of their family's history. The struggle among parents with wanting to both tell and not tell children of their family's history was equally intense. For many, the urge to tell their children was on the edge of speech, vacillating between the tip of the tongue the recesses of the throat. A secret that lives on the cusp of speech is sometimes released and spit out during seemingly uneventful moments. The spill then roams, without borders, altering the dynamics of a family in ways that cannot be anticipated.

Regina had been baptized and had been closely connected to the church. She had attended church every week with her father until she was in her early teens. At thirteen, she had an argument with her priest regarding the Holy Trinity and felt rejected by one of God's messengers. At fifteen, Regina told me that her life changed on an ordinary day while peeling potatoes with her mother. They were talking about recent news events, specifically the conflict created by Christian crosses that had just been installed at a convent near Auschwitz.[10] The crosses were visible to visitors of the concentration camp, which was just across the road.

Suddenly, said Regina, there was a silence in the room. It was a long silence that screamed to be heard. Still peeling potatoes, in a low voice close to a painful whisper, her mother chose that moment to tell her that she had been born a Jew. Her mother said that no one, including her husband, Regina's father, knew this secret. Regina was speechless for a moment and then demanded to know more. But her mother refused to continue the conversation. Spilled, regurgitated, the secret was spit up and soaked in by Regina. She was drenched in it as she lapped it up and absorbed it like mother's milk.

A moment's spill changed Regina's life. For months she could not grasp who she was and felt uncomfortable with an identity that was foreign to her. "I had problems trying to understand who I was, having a Jewish mother," she said.

She spoke to a friend, who had also recently discovered her Jewish roots. Together, they decided that they should learn Hebrew. They began meeting in the Jewish theater in Warsaw for lessons. She kept the fact that she was learning Hebrew a secret from her family for a long time. She also secretly participated in the Holy Days. Ultimately, Regina decided to be honest with her friends and family about her newfound identity and even began to keep a kosher home. I asked her to describe her identity. She replied:

> I basically feel myself being part of Man, second as a woman, third as a Jewish woman, and fourth as a Polish- Jewish woman. I think that, of course, it is all connected. To be a human being is the basis for the rest. For a long time I had problems with my Polish-Jewish identification, but finally I feel my answer is that I am both 100 percent Polish and 100 percent Jewish, not 50–50. I like Judaism very much and it helps me to integrate everything else. It feels like a wise religion that helps to ask questions and look for answers of a basic existential nature.

Her parents were angry at the idea of her admitting to being a Jew, and further horrified at her decision to become an observant Jew. Gradually, however, her mother was less and less against her decision, and told her that she was proud that she was more connected with her "line." Regina's mother accepted her choice but was saddened that Regina decided to move out of the house in order to be able to lead a more observant Jewish life. She was also afraid for her daughter's future as a Jew in Poland.

Her father had stopped talking to her when she took her younger brother to Rychwald for a weekend. He became enraged that she would take his Christian son to a Jewish camp. She responded by saying that his son was also her brother, and she was sharing with him part of his heritage. Her father became estranged from both Regina and his wife, telling them that if his wife had acted the way his daughter had, he would never have married her.

The moment he said this, recounted Regina, there was silence in the room. Regina shook her head, and with tears running down her face, expressed her heartbreak. She had thought that religion brought a family together, but by following her heritage she realized she would need to be prepared to lose her family.

Separation from her father was excruciating. Since he refused to talk about the subject, Regina attempted to communicate with him through letters. She explained her reasons for wanting to explore her Jewish tradition and stated that she had not tried to separate her brother from her father. She felt close to her brother and wanted him to have the opportunity and the time to explore both traditions, for his own clarity, since he was also the son of a Jewish mother.

Her father replied that he would never forgive her for having taken her brother to the Jewish camp. He wanted his children to follow Christian traditions and to teach these traditions to their future children. He said that she had become a stranger, and he would never accept her choice. She said that she tried to change his opinion in the letters but was not successful.

Regina mentioned that her father always considered people of different religions to be foreigners, so to him, she was a stranger. She was "the other." He became alienated both from his daughter, who was exploring her Jewish roots, and his wife, who had them. The secret, brought to the surface and expressed, led to the disintegration of a long-time marriage and altered the dynamics of an entire family.

Stefan told me that he became aware of being Jewish during a wave of anti-Semitism that swept Poland during the 1968 nationwide purge of Jews. He was seventeen and his parents, who were professors, began experiencing "trouble" at their university. Ultimately, his father was asked to step down from his position at the university because he was a Jew.

Stefan thought that he knew his history and religion. When his questions regarding his parents "trouble" were answered directly for the first time, he realized how much he had never been told. He learned that his father had spent some time in the Warsaw ghetto, escaping and returning several times. All of his father's family had perished. His father's mother and sister were told by the Germans that they would be freed for a large sum of money. After paying, they were put on trains never to be seen again. He assumed that they were transferred to death camps.

I asked about his mother's family. He said that his maternal grandmother was married to a German officer and had two daughters, one of whom was his mother. Although his grandfather was pressured to leave his Jewish wife, he did not. At the end of the war, the Russians came and took his grandfather to a Russian camp. Although his wife tried desperately to have him released, he sadly spent the rest of his life incarcerated. Stefan's mother met his father as he was returning from the Polish army in 1943 and they married. Stefan was born in 1951.

Stefan said he felt robbed at having learned about his family's true story so late. He had known his maternal grandmother was married to a German. But he never knew that she was a Jew who needed her German husband to save and protect her from harm. To Stefan, it was like peeling an onion, one tearful layer at a time.

Stefan had not felt harmed being Jewish, because he hadn't

known that he was. When asked at school whether he was a Jew, he would honestly say that he was not. He offered: "Not being told was a mistake, yet not knowing gave me additional safety, which was lost once I knew. I feel that being a Jew in Poland is not easy. One is never considered a real Pole. It is like having a double identity, which is stressful and difficult." Having been diligent and having worked hard, Stefan, like his father, had become a professor. Although he "felt robbed" about not knowing his heritage, he found it difficult, like his father, to tell his children about theirs.

When his daughter was fifteen, she came home from school with anti-Semitic jokes. He sensed the opportunity to tell her and seized it. He asked her whether she knew any Jews. She looked at him quizzically, as if he should have known that she did not. He then told her that indeed she did, because she was one. He explained that the family was Jewish and told her all that he knew. She was shocked, asking for the story to be repeated again and again. To this day she has been trying to adapt. It was then necessary to tell his son, whose response was more receptive.

Stefan thought that "knowing" has made them lose their innocence. As a parent, he knows that he is not alone in not having told his children earlier. He thinks that other parents are also afraid of harming their children in some way by having them know anything about being Jewish.

Sensing his ambivalence, I asked, "Do you identify yourself more as a Jew, Christian, or Pole?"

Stefan replied, "I'm certainly a Pole as I am deep in the culture. It is also my language, my first language, which is important to me. I would like to learn more about being Jewish. It made quite a strong impression on me to find out, but I was never anti-Semitic, so I didn't have that problem."

I asked him what he meant by "strong impression." He said he should have known much earlier that he was a Jew. He believes it is important to know family history and tradition. He says he somehow lost time by not knowing: "I only knew myself superficially."

I met Tanya, a kitchen helper at Rychwald, on a warm day. I was thirsty and had gone to the kitchen to get a glass of bottled water. (No one drank water from the faucet; vegetables were even washed with bottled water.) I asked her for water and she offered me tea. I would later learn she often gives more of herself than asked.

I was happy to see that within a day of our first meeting, I found her name on the roster given to me. She was willing to tell her story. She told me that she had never been baptized and had never gone to church. When she questioned as a young girl why her family was not religious like others, she was told that her father was a military officer and that they did not go for political reasons.

Tanya was in her thirties when her husband died, leaving her with two young children. They had been married in a civil ceremony, as she was a nonpracticing Catholic and he was an atheist. In searching through his papers after his death, she discovered that his family was Jewish. She was not anti-Semitic but was terribly upset to think of her children having to face the future as "mixed."

Her mother then took the opportunity to tell her that her family was Jewish as well, and that she had known the same was true of her son-in-law. She had known that her future grandchildren would be Jewish, even though neither of their parents did. Her mother said that she was trying to protect her daughter in case of "future problems." Since she was blond and blue eyed, she would never be suspected of being a Jew.

Tanya spent a lot of time talking to her mother but lacked the courage to ask detailed questions. Just as she was ready to know more, her mother died. She did know certain facts about her family, though. For instance, her father had been discharged from military service. At the time, she never really understood why but came to learn it was because others in the military had discovered he was a Jew. Tanya learned that he had hidden in Warsaw during the war and that his family had been Orthodox Jews from Lvov.

Tanya's mother had lived in the Warsaw ghetto for three years with her family, all of whom were eventually sent to concentration camps and perished. She remained and was saved somehow by a Polish family who deposited her in a Jewish orphanage after the war. Tanya asked her mother whether she had ever searched for her parents after the war. Her mother said that she thought that if anyone had survived, they would have come back and found her. She was raised in an orphanage and had no real sense of family.

Tanya, sensing her mother's frailty, stopped asking questions. Before she died, her mother did show her a picture of the orphanage and Tanya was able to ask her why she hadn't left Poland. Her mother told her that she was afraid to leave and that she had met and married a Catholic Pole. She was able to say that she had asked her Catholic husband not to bury her in a Catholic cemetery. Her husband had complied before they divorced and had bought two plots in a Jewish cemetery. Tanya thought this was beautiful and very tolerant. I asked her whether she thought that there were many Jews buried in Catholic cemeteries. Indeed, she thought there were Jews "hiding" in Catholic cemeteries.

After learning the truth, she decided she wanted her children raised in a culture that supports Judaism and began working hard to try to send them to Israel. She knew she would miss them terribly but believed this was the only way her children would be able to truly know their heritage. Tanya also educated herself about the small local Jewish community. She made herself available to help with cooking meals for the holidays. She was committed to starting a Jewish tradition for her children, hoping it would serve future generations. When Tanya's son asked her whether he should tell friends that he would be going to Israel, she told him to tell the truth. She told him that not only Jews go to Israel. His fear about telling others only strengthened Tanya's resolve to send her children to a place where they didn't need to fear being Jews.

I had much to learn about how discovery created changes in family dynamics.

Tadeusz told me that he was forty. Although his father never admitted to being Jewish outright, Tadeusz recalled that when he was a child letters often arrived from Israel in Hebrew, which his father was able to read. He noticed other things growing up, but he never raised the topic. He said his father died when he was sixteen and that he is just starting to discuss it with his mother now. She won't tell him whether she is Jewish, but he continues to ask.

I asked him whether he went to church as a child. He said that it was a very difficult time in Poland and remembered not going to church until he was twelve. He had found letters from his father's family stating that it would be a good idea for the family to start going to church. Indeed, he recalled his parents started taking him and his sister to church in 1968. Eventually, he was able to trace his father's first wife's grandson, who lived in France and was able to fill in some gaps in the family's history.

His father was the youngest of a large family with a dozen children, most of whom were lost in the war. His father was married before the war and had two children, a son and a daughter. His wife and son did not survive the war, but his daughter survived, went to France, married, and had two children. It was her son who was helping Tadeusz learn about his family.

He discovered that the family had been assimilated Jews who celebrated the Sabbath and Holy Days. His grandfather had been a teacher. His father, the youngest, supported the entire family. He began by privately teaching the sons of wealthy Poles. He then went to medical school in Vienna and returned to his family in Krakow just before the war.

The Germans came to Krakow and were in the process of starting a ghetto when Tadeusz's father escaped. He enlisted in the Russian army and served as a doctor. After the war, he convinced a general to let him come back to Krakow. Upon his return, he discovered that nearly his entire family had perished in the ghetto.

Tadeusz made a decision to rekindle the family tradition and lead a Jewish life. However, he had to rethink the difficulties he would have in the future if he chose to remain in Poland. Highly educated and in a highly visible position, he would need to work on the Sabbath. He did not live near enough to a synagogue for weekly attendance and wanted to be religious without it causing constant hardship. Therefore, he thought leaving Poland was the best religious choice, although it meant that he would need to leave his parents behind.

The flower of Judaism would grow outside of Poland, but since the buds had started in Poland, it would mean "cutting the bouquet to bring it elsewhere." It was a conflict between being able to lead a Jewish life, and leaving friends and family. But Tadeusz desperately wanted to live in a place where he could celebrate the Sabbath openly, without consequence. It would be a difficult decision.

Difficulties did not rest only with those who pursued Jewish traditions. Those who chose to continue leading life as it was before discovery needed to find ways to integrate this newfound information. There were those who maintained the secret, and those who did not. It was easier for some than for others.

Janus had grown up knowing somehow that he would become a priest, and indeed he had. He had a very close relationship with his mother, who was a simple and very honest woman. When he lived at home, he would read newspaper articles to her, because she had never learned to read. They both enjoyed their time together. He noted on several occasions that his mother seemed to have tears in her eyes when he read articles regarding Jews. He asked if they were Jewish, but she remained silent. He was shaken by how the emptiness cried out to him.

Years later, when his mother was hospitalized with a serious illness, he asked her again. This time, she did not hesitate to tell him: he was adopted. His birth mother and father were Jews who loved him very much. They had begged her, their Christian neighbor who lived next door, to rescue their beautiful infant by taking him as her own, before they were taken away. She remembered that his birth mother had said before she was taken off to a death camp: "You are a devout Catholic. You believe in Jesus, who was a Jew. Save this Jewish baby for the Jew in whom you believe. One day he will grow up to be a priest."

With the unfolding of this secret, she produced a photo of his birth mother. He took this precious gift from the only mother that he knew. Looking at the photo, he was astonished to see that he bore a striking resemblance to her. He had always quietly wondered why he did not resemble anyone else in his family. Although he honored his birth mother and her religion, he identified strongly with being a Catholic priest and wanted to remain one. Nevertheless, he knew it would take time to integrate what he had just learned about his past with his present identity.

Unlike others, he decided to become vocal about his discovery. In turn, the Polish world treated him with the respect given a priest. He knew that his honesty about discovery might help society accept others who discover in the future. He has found additional comfort by telling his story all over the world and by teaching tolerance at a Christian university in Poland.

Magda's mother was a bank officer who learned about Rychwald when Rabbi Schudrich approached the bank for an extension of credit for the summer camp. She asked for literature about the camp and thought it interesting enough to bring home to show her husband, whom she thought had some Jewish roots. Indeed, she was correct, but he had not wanted to expose that truth to their children, even though they were grown and had children of their own. Most of the Jewish side of the family had perished, and he was afraid that history would be repeated. She thought the secret should be told, but he resisted.

In a similar case, a Catholic woman in her thirties learned while sitting at the bedside of her father, who had been hospitalized with a serious condition. As he lay dying, he asked for his prayer shawl and prayer book and then began to chant in Yiddish. The daughter was stunned, paralyzed. Before she could respond, he died. She told no one about what had happened, not even her husband or siblings, and held the secret for nine years before she dared speak of it. She remembered feeling very close to her father before the incident but said she perceived him as "alien" the moment his hidden identity emerged. I wondered whether she would ever allow herself to accept her father in a loving way—and as a Jew.

Jacek's ailing father, a farmer, had summoned his three sons to discuss how his farm should be divided after his death. He told Jacek that although he loved him like a son, he was not his real father. During the war, the farmer had found Jacek wandering in the snow with hardly any clothes on. He was clutching the hand of an older child, a girl. Both were frostbitten. He recognized that the children would soon die of exposure if left alone. Another passerby took the girl but was unwilling to take the boy as it was a danger to save any Jew, but more dangerous to save a boy who was tagged as a Jew by circumcision. The farmer brought the boy home and took him in.

At his deathbed, he told Jacek that land went only to "blood," so it must be passed on to his two brothers. He was sorry that he could not give him any land for his future. Jacek felt abandoned and desperate. He said that working the land was the only life that he knew and that his family was courteous but no longer his family. He did not know where to go or what to do. He wanted help in finding any family member who might have survived, but he could only recall the name of a pet and had no recollection of a distinct family name. His felt his only hope was in an advertisement he had placed in the newspaper, inquiring about the little girl whose hand he had held in the snow more than fifty years earlier.

A lifetime had gone by during my two weeks in Poland. Going back home, the difference was not so much in time as in dimension. The secrets that had been exposed in Poland, and all the problems associated with them, imposed a heavy, regressed, primitive thought process. I was relieved when the plane was able to lift off the ground. I wondered who would do the hand holding now, as discoveries continued to be made. I had come hoping to do research that would help my groups at home and had found myself wanting to be useful here, where it all began.

Life in the United States felt calm and safe yet ordinary and dull compared to the intensity of Poland. During the next several weeks I transcribed the audiotapes from my interviews and wrote a letter to Rabbi Schudrich, thanking him for his help with the entire process and making recommendations based on the data I had collected. I stated that although individuals should be encouraged to explore their Jewish roots, unless they received psychological support, they were at increased risk for experiencing conflict with their families. If an individual's exploration of Judaism was perceived as dangerous within a family, for example, the conflict created could put the family at risk of falling apart. I noted that such conflict is not conducive to building a sound Jewish community. Rabbi Schudrich called soon after, stating that he recognized the problem, could see the pitfalls, and asked me to come back to Poland to discuss ideas for a support strategy. I accepted.

7 Forbidden Knowledge

Once more the plane was packed with people speaking Polish. This time I didn't expect them to know me. There had been a shift. The language had become associated with my recent experience in Poland. The memories of my mother and her tongue remained more personal, more primitive, something that required no translation. I knew I needed to develop a strategic plan that would be effective and decided to first learn how the mental health professionals in Warsaw viewed this unfolding phenomenon.

I made arrangements to meet an analyst who had recently begun working with Holocaust survivors. The introduction was to take place at "Twarda," the name commonly used for the Lauder Foundation. It is the name of the street on which both the foundation and the synagogue are located and translates as "difficult." The foundation's building is situated in the midst of a pleasant grassy area in the center of the downtown business district.

Nina looked friendly. She had a twinkle in her brown eyes, accented slightly by the bangs cut just above the brow. Although in her thirties, she appeared younger. She suggested with a sweep of the hand that we go for a walk. The long skirt she wore suggested a soft manner, while our conversation revealed her strong commitment and dedication to work that others were afraid to do. Speaking with a well-educated psychiatrist and psychoanalyst helped to clarify the situation for me. She raised an issue I hadn't considered: treating Jews for their problems in private practice was one thing, but a public support group could bring unwanted attention to the professionals involved and adversely affect their careers. Nina knew that this fear was not completely rational, but it would take a while to change.

Nina told me that her father was Jewish and that she felt neither Jewish nor Christian. She was worried about the confusion this created in her children. It had taken courage for her to work with survivors. She explained that it had not been easy for her to enter the building that housed the office where she treated survivors, as those inside were known for "helping Jews."

I asked whether it would be possible to speak to other members of the mental health community. She said yes and very graciously suggested having a small diner party where I would have the opportunity to socialize with local mental health professionals.

Professionals who came to the party seemed very engaged in their work with patients. Professional similarities and differences were discussed. I said that I had wondered what would happen to the families who were struggling with discovery if they were not aided. They asked me how I would help those with dual Jewish-Catholic identities. I replied by saying there is a small but similar community in the United States, the sons and daughters of those who had emigrated from Poland and other parts of Europe. Support groups had been very helpful for them, but the protocols were specific to a different country and culture.

There was interest in the group modality, especially since it had not been possible to hold such group meetings under the closed Communist system. Although everyone admitted that family difficulties were a problem for those who had discovered, no one had openly addressed the situation. One professional asked why I thought I could tell them what to do. I replied that I wasn't there to tell them what to do but to help empower them, that is, if they wanted my help. I asked for people to get in touch with me privately if they were interested in doing group work. Several professionals approached me quietly, interested to know more. I was asked whether it was important to be Jewish to do this work, and I replied that the only credentials needed were proper training and experience.

With the possibilities of staff becoming available, I wanted to do research to see whether or not a group process would be accepted in Poland. I was invited to a Jewish self-help group that had been in existence for several years. This all-female group was comprised of friends who had known each other for many years and met privately once or twice monthly at someone's home. They shared individual issues as well as those relating to being Jewish. The group consisted of a dozen or so women, mostly professionals active in the small Jewish community. Knowing each other well, each was trusted to invite an outsider who needed help. Each had a turn in chairing the meetings. The evening that I joined them, the group was helping a friend's daughter who was upset that her Jewish identity had recently been exposed to her friends.

She had been walking across her university's campus with her closest friends. They had all known one another since grammar school and were laughing together. A girl who hardly knew her but had seen her at the Lauder Foundation said hello to her across the square and started to walk toward her with great enthusiasm. She felt paralyzed, knowing that this girl may refer to something Jewish while she was standing with her lifelong friends who had no idea that she was a Jew. Acting as if she didn't recognize her, the friendly girl reminded her that they had met at the Lauder Foundation. Frozen, she made the appropriate introductions. Her friends did not say anything unusual, so she was not sure that they had understood. She felt utterly exposed and ashamed. It made her angry that this girl could so easily "expose" her. She wanted the group to find a way to tell young people not to expose others as Jews outside of the Lauder Foundation. She felt ashamed that she had not chosen to tell her best friends that she was Jewish. They would be shocked to know that she was a Jew and probably disappointed in that she had not trusted them enough to tell them. Not feeling close to anyone Jewish, she now felt alienated from her best friends.

The group sympathized with her situation and told their own stories. One member, a mathematician, shared that she was jealous of everyone who wore a cross in full view. For years she had worn a Jewish Chai emblem around her neck, but hid it under her shirt. This emblem was chosen because it wasn't as obvious as a Star of David and not as easily recognized. After thinking about it she decided to wear it in full view. A woman at work asked her if it represented the symbol pi. She heard herself saying yes. These conversations brought out the ambivalence that many people had about telling others that they were Jews. *The decision to "try on" Judaism opened the possibility of exposure before some were ready for a personal commitment. Would open groups create more problems than they solved?*

Not knowing whether people would feel comfortable enough to ask questions in an open forum, I asked for an open meeting where I would discuss and answer questions regarding Jewish life in New York. An announcement was made inviting people to spend an evening at the Lauder Foundation to learn about Jewish issues in the United States. I wondered whether anyone would come, and whether I would understand the cultural process just as those in the room would no doubt struggle to understand my Polish. Chairs were placed in a circle, and approximately fifteen people came. I tried being as informative as possible.

By pure chance, one of the participants was a Holocaust survivor who became argumentative when a younger woman asked a question. The younger woman said that this was the kind of argument she often had with her mother, also a survivor. I recognized the opportunity to conduct a working dialogue "on the spot" between these two women. Both women addressed each other's complaints after I intervened by asking for clarification. The young woman was able to gain insight about her mother's behavior and thanked me after the meeting. The group seemed interested in watching the process unfold. This was the beginning of a religious identity group process in Warsaw. It was going to work!

The next step was to formulate a vision with realistic goals for the project, look for funding, and organize the teaching of staff. Much needed to be done in order to effectuate a working support group. It was important to uncover what was not known about this unique population. But for the moment, I needed to allow myself not to know and to proceed with the hope that the path would become clear, one step at a time.

Grant proposals were sent to various organizations. Most foundations were not interested in funding a project in Poland. One or two considered the project but asked that it be structured to provide quantifiable results. This would be a reasonable request for most studies but would be impossible in circumstances laden with secrecy.

The Lauder Foundation agreed to collaborate and give contributions in-kind. They would provide a meeting place for groups and needed supplies. Michael and I brainstormed about other possible avenues for funding. Steven Spielberg had recently been in Warsaw and was aware of the unfolding of Jewish roots there. Although his foundations did not generally contribute grants to Poland, with his generosity, the Righteous Persons Foundation agreed to jump start the project. They funded the training portion of the project and gave partial support for activities in the second year.

The next several months were spent preparing material for the teaching of group process. And a one-week winter camp was planned for future staff.

8 "Broken Chain": The Work Begins

The long flight was useful in putting my thoughts together. The hours spent traveling by car and train, between the Lauder Foundation in Warsaw and camp Rychwald in Bielsko Biyala, were accented with smiles and words of welcome from known caretakers and drivers. It was the same long trip, but in a different season. It was winter, cold and snowy. I had heard on the news that several people had succumbed to frostbite. For some reason I had an irrational fear of dying of cold, as if I would be forced to walk for miles in the snow. Although I was intimidated by the frost, the journey went well. I arrived at camp a day before the arrival of the four potential staff members who had accepted my invitation for a group weekend. I will refer to them as Magda, Anya, Alex, and Marianna.

I spent the day checking work accommodations and saying hello to people that I had seen in camp during my summer stay. The next day staff members started to arrive and were shown to their rooms. We were to meet formally after dinner.

It was Friday evening, the beginning of the Sabbath, and dinner was normally served after evening prayer. There was an area set aside for young women to light Sabbath candles if they so wished. Magda approached and asked if she could try lighting candles. Being quite surprised, I invited her to do so. She said she needed help, for although she was more than thirty, she had never done so before, and didn't know what to do. She tentatively followed my lead, as if not sure that she should be participating in this ritual, and lit the candles while repeating the prayer. I later discovered that she was still not sure whether or not she was Jewish as her mother continued to deny it. I had asked prospective group leaders to come for the weekend to experience group work as part of training, to better understand the process, and to get to know one another. Additionally, I wanted each leader to experience being in a Jewish camp. These potential leaders needed to understand their individual responses to this experience and to recognize their own religious identity conflicts before they could lead a group in an authentic manner. I only hoped that I wouldn't miss many cues.

The staff and I were seated with foreign guests who were interested in knowing more about the "Jewish experience" in Poland. These future leaders needed to lower their guard enough to answer the questions of foreigners who had little idea about the personal struggle they were experiencing from just sitting among Jews, never mind from being treated as if they were Jews. Guests were from the United States, Israel, Germany, and other parts of Europe. They were impressed by the enthusiasm with which they were met, but were unaware of the difficulties imposed by their intrusive questions, particularly toward those who had lived within a Communist state and were presently caught in an identity crisis fueled by varying degrees of external hatred and internal self-hatred.

Guests from Western Europe and the United States spoke positively about the experience of going "home" to the place of their known heritage, whether in Eastern Europe or elsewhere. In contrast, many of the Poles at the table were just beginning to discover their own true heritage and did not feel comfortable "at home." Those whose families had left before the war had maintained their heritage. Those who had stayed lost their heritage and often their families. What irony.

Guests were asked about Jewish life where they lived. They answered spontaneously, not feeling a need to guard their association to Judaism, since most lived in parts of the world that were more tolerant to religious differences. It was an eye opening experience for both sides of the table.

After dinner, Magda, Anya, Alex, Marianna, and I settled down to our professional group meeting. I asked them to start by describing their impressions of their journey to camp. Magda and Anya, who traveled together, mentioned how they had talked about helping others with Jewish identity problems, but were shocked to find themselves trying to describe the camp's location to the cab driver without using the word "Jew." They cringed when he referred to it as the "Jewish" place. All four staff members had familial connections to Judaism but were anxious because they felt as though they did not know enough about the issues Jews faced or about Judaism as a religion.

Issues regarding being Jewish, or partly Jewish, started to spill immediately. Most had never been among Jews. After working for several hours, I asked whether anyone wanted to stop for a break. Magda said that her father told her that she only looked like a "Jew" when she was tired. He had also told her not to express herself with the use of her hands. I wondered whether she was afraid that spending so much time among "Jews" would forever make her look noticeably like a Jew. Anya said that her mother was a doctor who had forbidden her to cough when she had a cold. During the war, when in hiding, coughing endangered the entire group. There was a constant fear that a child would cough, causing the group to be discovered and killed. That first day, the theme of hiding as a Jew was pronounced. Alex said that, in his family, the only survivors of the war were those who claimed to be Christian. Primitive fears were rising like bubbles and bursting at the surface, exposed, for each member of the group to see.

There was a curiosity forming in these professionals about their own backgrounds. We worked out a schedule that would allow them to attend programs of interest to them, enabling us to do our teamwork while meeting their personal needs.

At the end of the weekend, staff members seemed relieved at having been able to speak openly about their fears and doubts. Thankfully, groups were a minimum of six months away. I promised to send literature and taped sessions of group work so they might become more familiar with the process. For the present, we needed to develop a promotional strategy for the coming year.

After the weekend, I had the opportunity to conduct an open group for several days. Michael had announced group meetings would be held for anyone who wanted to discuss issues relating to Judaism. The first day, at the appointed hour, several young adults came, but they all thought group process simply meant they should come as a group, and that I would then see them individually! Open expression of sensitive subjects among people other than trusted friends was unusual and needed to be cultivated. We rephrased the announcement and in the following days more people came. They worked well in group process.

One of the adolescent themes we explored was the pain of wanting to tell a "best friend" about Jewish roots but being afraid of rejection. There was a discussion about how known Jews were treated in school, and how difficult it would be to put oneself in that situation. Jews often didn't have friends at school and teachers were often "not nice" to them. Many complained about friends using the colloquial expression, "You're doing that like a Jew," and feeling badly for not having the courage to tell them, "Maybe it's because I am!"

Another theme that came up was fear that self-disclosure of Judaism would jeopardize the entire family. Those wanting to tell others had been warned that it would "ruin the life" of all in the family. They spoke often about their frustrations regarding love. Some were in love with people who were not Jewish and needed to consider what their future would look like, particularly if raising children as Jews was important to them. Others claimed that they knew the few young "open" Jews in the community and did not foresee them as future romantic partners. It was like playing a game of musical chairs and knowing that there were not enough chairs.

There also was confusion regarding nationality. Was Judaism merely a religion? Or was it also a nationality equal to being a Pole? Must one choose between one or the other? The confusion dated to the 1921 Polish census, which allowed Jews to claim "Jewish" as a nationality. There were two non-Poles at the table who explained that in most other parts of the world religion had no bearing on one's nationality.

It was apparent how important it was for people to have a forum in which to discuss the conflicts and fears about the discovery of Jewish roots.

Group process had been found to be very suitable, effective, and helpful in the United States. However, there had been little or no experience with open group process in Poland, and trained leaders would need to be able to lead groups independently, with only outside supervision. From a clinical perspective we had little time, and the probability of success was somewhat low. I was encouraged, however, after I met a young couple from the camp on the train to Warsaw. They were in love and felt very lucky to have found each other. They said that finding one's true love is always a miracle, but the chances of a Jewish couple meeting in Poland was even a greater miracle. As I spoke to them about the possibility of support groups, they were very enthusiastic because they saw it as a potential means for social interaction among young Jews. There was a thirst to speak to others who had discovered Jewish roots in order to share insight about their future and that of the next generation, and they spoke of the sadness of feeling separated from their families.

On the flight home, I started planning the press releases and publicity. I would be returning to Warsaw for several scheduled interviews on radio and with major newspapers. This would be followed
by weekly advertisements inviting people to call in for information
about groups that would begin in the months ahead.

The staff was helpful in setting up interviews and discussing
strategy. Magda and Anya were helpful in finding an apartment for
me. Although enthusiastic about the idea of support groups, there
was a cultural difference between us. My suggestion to place an
advertisement in a highly publicized and well-distributed newspaper was met with disapproval. The staff was appalled with such
direct mainstream exposure, although they understood its necessi-
ty. I needed to listen and temper my direct manner so that I did not
overwhelm the people that I was trying to attract, and needed to
empower a staff that was courageous yet unsure.

Additionally, the project needed a name that sounded right both
in Polish and in English. After several attempts we agreed on
"Broken Chain," a reference to the interruptions and discontinuity
in family legacy created by war and its well-kept secrets. The advertisements stressed that prospective participants could remain
anonymous if they so chose by speaking with a leader over the
phone. Help was not contingent upon a face-to-face meeting.
Broken Chain sponsored the hotline and worked with a self-help
group called the Jewish Forum, which had formed years earlier and
met monthly to discuss Jewish affairs in a private and friendly environment. It was a good partnership for both sides, although the
local group had taken a chance in associating with a "foreign" one.

Soon, press, radio, and television interview requests started
coming in. The media naturally wanted to interview the leaders
who would be conducting the groups, particularly the Polish staff.
Staff members were pressured by their families to avoid all inter-

views and to avoid being publicly associated with the project, because they feared exposure would jeopardize the jobs of family members. Further, those who were parents were worried about how their children and grandchildren might be treated should they be "outed."

Programs were going to be held at the Lauder Foundation—the "Jewish place," as it was known—situated in the center of town next to the only synagogue in Warsaw. At first, leaders wanted pre-group interviews to be conducted in their private offices or clinics. I insisted that people who were trying to "come out" with their Jewish identity needed to be able to walk through the gates of a Jewish organization and not be kept in "hiding" by the professionals who were helping them to "come out." Although they agreed that in theory it was a good idea, they nevertheless expressed a fear of being seen walking into a "Jewish" place.

The next several months of training included developing the necessary protocols for the groups. Although funding would come more easily to a well-designed research project, I was told that even an anonymous paper and pencil questionnaire would scare away potential group members. I decided to listen to the advice of my well-educated staff. However, I did insist that prospective group members be interviewed prior to acceptance and that each member compose a family tree. The interviews were meant to ensure all members would benefit from group work. The formation of a family tree would serve as a visual chronicle of the losses and "holes" in one's lineage. "Seeing" the losses together with the leader would help create a bond between them and serve as a preamble to group work.

All staff members initially had a resistance to asking for family trees, arguing that although it had worked in the United States, it would not work in an anti-Semitic post-Communist state. Resistance subsided, however, when I asked for a staff volunteer to build a personal family tree in a meeting. All were surprised by the emotional impact and bonding raised by the mutual experience, and agreed to work in the same manner. Although we were working through problems in the group, I was concerned that the staff would not be able to handle unforeseen difficulties without the benefit of experience.

Time was quickly approaching, throwing the spotlight on Broken Chain. The publicity campaign was set to begin.

We immediately began receiving interest in the project. One of Warsaw's primetime television news programs even called the foundation and wanted a short interview from a group leader. The leader who had taken the call was to do the interview live but was having difficulty with a family member who had a high-profile job. This individual was afraid that people would connect the leader with her family and expose the family secret. Ultimately, the leader insisted on doing the interview but promised to be discreet. Even good news was complicated in Poland.

Our ad ran for thirteen weeks in two major newspapers. We determined that some people would need to see the ad a number of times before having the courage to call. It translated as follows:

Do you have Jewish Roots?
Is it your problem? Or secret?

The Jewish Forum Foundation is organizing support groups for people willing to talk with others about their feelings, difficulties, and hopes connected with Jewish roots. The meetings will be free and led by a psychotherapist. Applications to the groups starting in autumn in Warsaw are being accepted now.

We remind you that the Jewish hotline is active and one can always talk anonymously about problems connected with Jewish heritage, without obligation. "YOU DON'T HAVE TO FACE THESE PROBLEMS ALONE! "

Anticipating a large response, we worked out a schedule to ensure phones were covered at all times. The first week saw a diverse mix of interesting calls. Most people were nervous about telling their stories for the first time. Several calls were from people who believed that they were not really the children of their parents and that their birth parents were Jewish. The stories varied, but the callers all expressed feelings of shock, fear, and disbelief:

> "My mother told me that she was Jewish when she was told that she was dying, but she has since recovered and now claims that she was delusional."

> "Because of prevailing anti-Semitism I find myself also anti-Semitic. How do I get rid of it?"

> "I don't know who I am nor who I want to be. It is as if I exist on two sides of the river."

> "It is as if you had always thought of yourself as a woman, and discover that you are really a man."

People seemed to be relieved at finally being able to talk to someone, even if over the phone. Some wanted help in confirming whether or not they actually had Jewish roots. Several psychologists called wanting to be trained to do group work. There were several anti-Semitic calls, but not as many as expected.

The initial phase had begun. Staff felt comfortable enough to conduct interviews with supervision. I began spending seven to ten days a month in my rented apartment. In this way, once groups began, I would be able to supervise two out of four sessions each month. Setting roots, shopping, and cooking locally was a bigger commitment to the project than if I had resided in a hotel. It helped me to know how people lived in Warsaw on a daily basis.

When calls came in, individuals were not asked for personal data, such as last name or telephone number. This meant that if an appointment was made, the staff member would not be able to cancel, reschedule, or reconfirm a time. We found that most people came in for their appointments as scheduled, but that many were reluctant to set up an appointment the first time they called. Most called back two or more times before they felt comfortable enough to arrange a meeting. Many said that they had seen the ad in the paper for several weeks before calling. They needed this assurance that the group was stable.

People were very nervous about exploring for the first time, in the presence of others, what they knew about their Jewish heritage. The majority of individuals needed assistance with the family tree and were grateful to receive help when needed from the therapist. For the most part, they had not told anyone about their discoveries and had been afraid to do any investigating of their own. It seemed therapeutic for them to finally hear the fears and doubts of others and to have someone else listen to their own concerns in a safe and confidential environment.

Interestingly, the hotline received many calls from outside the Warsaw area. Indeed, there were a dozen people who traveled several hours by train in each direction for the interviews and for the hope that groups would eventually start closer to their homes. After groups began, one woman even traveled two hours each way every Tuesday evening to attend. She kept her group meetings a secret from her family until her husband confronted her, accusing her of having an affair!

Calls came in at all hours of the day and every day of the week. The pace was grueling for the therapists on phone duty. Thankfully, the calls were to a cell phone, which meant the therapists did not need to be tied to a desk. There were many people who called the hotline just to talk. Others were more willing to peel away at the skin of secrecy and speak openly about their discovery in a group setting. Generally speaking, the curiosity to meet others who had also discovered Jewish roots simply exceeded any anxiety they might have had. Those who were close enough to make the journey to central Warsaw were asked to commit to eight consecutive weekly sessions. They were told they would be able to commit to additional eight-week intervals if they liked. By October 1998, two eight-person groups had been formed and were set to begin their journey.

9 Facing Oneself and One Another

Group meetings were to be held in a quiet room on the ground floor of the Lauder Foundation. The room was equipped as a small gymnasium for the kindergarten class during morning hours. It had a private and clean appearance with wooden floors and two picture windows facing the rear of the building. Although it was too spacious for small groups, it allowed for privacy. A rug and several lamps were bought for use during group meetings to add warmth to a room overcome with stark overhead lighting. This attempt to provide a warm and safe setting was undercut by the armed guards stationed at the front entrance.

Initial group meetings were difficult yet had elements of spontaneity. Group members gathered outside, acting as if they needed to be invited to come in. The first groups did not enter at once and needed guidance to be seated. After the first session members learned to come in and take a seat, but as one therapist put it, "People were sitting and waiting like at the dentist's office." This was partly a function of the novelty of such a gathering in Poland, and partly a function of the insecurity felt among the participants.

The therapists started by asking for first name introductions to ease into the discussion. Surprisingly, several members began to speak spontaneously about Jewish issues immediately after introducing themselves. Familiar themes emerged: some weren't sure whether they should tell their children about their discovery, and others feared anti-Semitism and being attacked walking into a "Jewish place." But all expressed relief at having a place to be able to talk about "it" with others. While some felt uncomfortable in both a synagogue and church, feeling as though they belonged in neither, they all felt as though they belonged in this group.

Members had been aware of anti-Semitism and may have even been anti-Semitic themselves before discovery, but they weren't sure how it would feel to have such hatred directed at themselves. Such feelings of persecution were shocking for people who had been raised Catholic in a country with a Catholic majority. Several members reluctantly admitted to circling the building several times and entering only when they were sure that they had not been seen. Most were afraid to tell their spouses and children.

Neither the world nor the people around them had changed. Rather, a revealed secret, which had been for so long uncovered, had changed their entire lives. Anti-Semitic friends unknowingly created an atmosphere in which open discussion about having Jewish roots seemed impossible. Members talked about not knowing how to respond to anti-Semitism. They were afraid they'd expose themselves if they somehow overreacted to it.

Several members felt badly about being Jewish and wished they could forget their discovery. Not liking Jews made it very difficult to admit to being one. One member who was raised Catholic and believed in the Holy Trinity thought it was too much to ask of herself to think about being another religion. Another felt that she had a debt to pay, as her parents had been hiding who they were and she felt the need to go back to their heritage. A woman responded angrily saying that whatever she decided to do, the next generation would probably need to join its own group for religious confusion.

One woman started to cry. She had a conflict about telling her son the truth. If she told him that he was a Jew, he would need to lie in school in order to feel safe. She asked the group, "How could you expect a child to be proud of his heritage and at the same time tell him to keep it a secret so that he'll be safe?"

The last five minutes of each session were always reserved for reactions to the group. For example, in the first session, many stated that they had never uttered the words "I am a Jew," so they all decided to say those words out loud.

At one later session a woman who had told her son that he was Jewish didn't know how to help him find meaning as a Jew, since she herself didn't feel like a Jew: "I feel empty, and I don't know what to transmit to my son." Several members had told only one member of the family their secret, either a child or a spouse, which entangled another person in a secret "without meaning." Over the next several weeks, people started to feel more comfortable at the meetings. Although still afraid of being beaten in the courtyard of a "Jewish place," most felt less anxious within the building and within their group. Members became more curious while walking through the halls to their sessions and noticed posters about upcoming Jewish events. They started asking questions regarding holidays and, although afraid of not knowing how to act in a synagogue, wanted to know more.

Talk about history and the positive values of Jewish family roots started to come forward. However, the voices would flip from positive to negative quite easily. There were discussions about Jews behaving like victims by submitting to the ghetto and not dying in dignity; in other instances, Jews were called the victimizers who killed Christ. One woman reported that she was taught growing up to always prepare for the worst. She said she didn't understand why until she discovered her family's hidden Jewish roots. She felt much better knowing and felt closer to her parents because of it. She thought it more important to feel integrated with the past, even if the current circumstances proved to be more difficult. Another member reported that in her family it didn't seem important to plan for life, for the future. Life was seen as precarious with everything likely to be lost regardless of how you lived it. Upon discovery, she realized this feeling was based on her family's experience in the Holocaust. Indeed, the Holocaust was an important topic to group members, who only with discovery were able to connect to it emotionally. The members began to feel empathy and sadness for the traumas endured by the Jewish community.

After several weeks, a man expressed frustration because he couldn't figure out a way to tell his wife that he was Jewish. A woman responded by saying that she had been able to tell her two children but also had not been able to tell her husband. Another woman added that she was able to tell her husband but was afraid to tell her in-laws. Her husband told her that he didn't like Jews and thought that his family would feel the same way.

The therapist leading the group intervened, saying that there seemed to be much fear about what would happen to relationships after family members learned about discoveries of Jewish roots. The conversation turned to marriages being built on lies, and the continuation of those lies to young children. One member asked whether there would be groups extended for children of group members. Members felt overwhelmed with the burden of knowing and telling. Several members remembered feeling different growing up and were anxious about overprotecting their children now that they knew.

One woman had felt stifled by her father and never understood why. He would hardly allow her to leave the house. She hadn't realized what her mother meant when she would say to him with disgust: "What do you know about the war, you spent it under floorboards!" This woman thought that overprotecting children was a Jewish trait brought on by the war. She also felt as though she herself had spent her life "under floorboards" and needed to free herself. A male member responded by saying that he didn't think such a generality was true, because his mother didn't notice what he did and didn't seem to take care of him particularly well. He thought she was so depressed that nothing mattered. He speculated that perhaps she felt so out of control and afraid of the future that she believed nothing she did could protect him, her only child.

The groups seemed to be having a profound impact on its members. Ideas that had been dormant were coming closer to the surface, faster than expected, opening conflicts along the way. One woman's adolescent daughter came home after having seen *Schindler's List* and looked at herself in the mirror, asking her mother whether she had Jewish roots. The mother denied it but went into her room and started to cry. She had wanted to tell her daughter but was afraid of what her husband would say. She approached her husband with the idea of telling their daughter, but he was very much against it. He said that they were protecting her by not telling her, as she would probably feel neither Polish nor Jewish if she knew. "She would feel like nobody," he said. To this, she replied, "You mean she would be a nobody like me?"

The group wondered what was holding the mother back, what prevented her from telling her daughter. While responding to their questions, the woman had a realization: her fear centered around her husband and doubts about him. She questioned whether he would have hidden her—saved her—during the war. This thought had a profound effect on her; she wasn't sure what this would mean for her twenty-year-old marriage. The room went silent. It became apparent that realizations brought to light within the group process could change the course of lives, for good and bad.

A member announced that he had told seven people that he was Jewish. He had not yet found the courage to tell his girlfriend, although he had not found it difficult to tell her that he was an alcoholic. Another woman decided to use her new Jewish identity to help her get out of a signed agreement. She had leased office space that she no longer wanted. Breaking the lease meant she would be charged with heavy penalties for early termination. Instead, she decided to put a Star of David on the wall. This made the landlord uncomfortable, and he asked her to leave. As a result, she incurred no penalties.

Members of the group also expressed curiosity about Jewish

events, but most did not feel "Jewish enough" to partake in them. One woman said that she and her son had begun taking Hebrew lessons. He started to wonder if any of his friends were hiding their Jewish roots from him, just as he was hiding his roots from them. She forbid him to ask anyone. Another woman mentioned that her husband was starting to get suspicious about her whereabouts each week when she came to the group sessions.

One man integrated all the themes under discussion by saying that he would have to change everything in order to be Jewish. He said that the group had helped him crystallize his position and he would need to decide what to do next. Several of the women had gone to a lecture about keeping a kosher kitchen and talked about all the trouble that they would have to go through to do so, from throwing away their pots to cooking for a Christian mother-in-law. The underlying question all asked was whether they would have to throw away being a Pole in order to be a Jew.

All wished to become more informed about the Holocaust and family members who had perished. Fear cropped up in different ways: one woman was afraid to take a taxi from the group meeting as the driver would know where she had been, while another woman feared that she would not be accepted as a Jew in Jewish circles or in temple. Another member was afraid of becoming dependent on the group. One member continued to take his son to church because he felt spiritually barren and wanted his son to have the opportunity to continue believing in something. A female member responded by saying that her Jewish mother had raised her to be Catholic in the best way that she knew, yet it was a dead and false way, which was not helpful to her.

On the positive side, the member who had not told his girlfriend that he was a Jew finally told her. He was very happy to report that she was not upset and that the relationship had not been ruined. One woman said that she wished her father would be able to tell her mother that he was a Jew. He lived outside of Warsaw and became very fearful when his daughter told him about the group. He was sure that lists of members' names were being kept, and he was afraid both for her and for himself.

There was a book fair in the building before one session, and members found themselves studying the books available. They came into group talking about the fact that there had been little available material about Judaism after the 1968 purge of Jews, but that the information was beginning to return. During the purge, most references to Jews and Judaism had been deleted from Polish texts. For example, one encyclopedia claimed that 6 million Poles had been killed in World War II, but made no mention of Jews.

As the first two groups were finishing their eight-week sessions, I was in Poland to supervise and to discuss future strategy. Christmas was approaching, and rather than risk members feeling as though they were splitting religious loyalties, we decided not to begin a new round of sessions until after the New Year. All expressed their desire to remain in the group. Indeed, the process had already begun to positively affect some of their lives.

At the first meeting after the break, a woman who had been unable to tell her husband that she was Jewish revealed that she had finally found a way to tell him. Having done so, she said she felt as though a stone had been lifted from her heart. She said she had bought a candelabrum for Chanukah and began to light the candles in front of him. When he asked what she was doing, she said she turned to him and simply said that she was a Jew.

She had found out about her Jewish roots a year into their marriage, when she learned about them at her mother's deathbed. Her husband listened to her story and responded with great empathy. He commented on how difficult it must have been for her to have kept this secret for so long. Together they spoke about whom they could tell in the family and decided together not to tell anyone. She was very proud of herself, however, and was heartened by the support she had received from her husband. Indeed, her appearance had even changed. Whereas before she had dressed in dull gray shades, she began to dress in colorful clothes.

The group responded with support, though with a bit of envy. The capacity to tell, and responses to telling, had become competitive. Generally, friends and family responded to revelations of one's secret either with acceptance, an anti-Semitic remark, or the words: "What's the big deal? You're still the same person."

In one of the following sessions, several of the women revealed they had attended a seminar together at the synagogue. Although afraid to ask questions, they thought that some people who had attended were not any "more advanced" than they were, and perhaps not even Jewish. Two members had been taking Hebrew lessons. It seemed as if their Jewish identities were becoming more pronounced. I thought about their courage and wondered about the future for Jews in Poland

The woman who had not been able to tell her daughter that she was Jewish related one of her daughter's dreams to the group. She said that her daughter had told her she dreamt that she was Jewish. The mother sighed and said that even though her mother had been able to tell her when she had asked, she was not as brave as her mother and was still unable to do the same.

One of the men said that his mother had never told him fully that she was a Jew, and he had wavered between really wanting to know and wanting the question to disappear. Perhaps the daughter wanted reassurance that she was not Jewish, he suggested. Another woman talked about having not known as a child, and only feeling whole once her father had told her the truth. Hearing the others speak, one man was moved enough to consider telling his own child in the near future.

Another man who was childless said that he was struggling internally with his Jewish and Polish "parts" and had a hard time imagining what it must be like to also struggle with whether or not to tell a child. He said that he often felt depressed when trying to understand his Jewish background. He came from a well-to-do family, had been successful himself, and had no external personal pressures to worry about. His great grandfather had been a Hasid, and both his mother and father were Jewish, but they divorced when he was young. His father remarried a Polish Gentile and his half-sisters never knew that their father was a Jew.

When his father died, he was buried in a Catholic cemetery with a cross over his grave. His uncle on his father's side insisted that this be so because he didn't want anyone to know that the family was Jewish. When he was younger, his father had told him that one hundred family members had been killed for being Jews, and that only he and his brother had survived. He felt as if his heritage had been buried in an unknown grave.

Two women talked about how they had not been able to bring themselves to read any material relating to the Holocaust, even after it had become available. Another woman said that she was consumed by the stories of the war and could not stop reading. She herself was conflicted because she realized that her parents would not have met if not for the Holocaust and that she would not have been born. Additionally, several members had been to a lecture about Judaism and were told that a baptized person could never be a Jew. Everyone wondered how this could be and thought that perhaps they had misunderstood. They said they felt just as rejected by this Jewish lecturer as they would by anti-Semites.

Questions were asked about the next cycle. The group leader replied by saying that the vision was for people to stay until they felt ready to leave. Everyone said that they would like to continue.

10 Integrating the Pieces

At the beginning of the next cycle, the woman who had avoided telling her daughter about her Jewish roots told her husband that she planned to do so during the next school vacation. Her husband was strongly against telling her and refused to discuss it further. She told the group at length how angry she was with him, calling him anti-Semitic. The group asked her to reflect on her anger. They pointed out that he loved his daughter, too, and was perhaps concerned about her future.

This led to a discussion about what it meant to be both a Pole and a Jew. Everyone agreed that they loved the warm and familiar streets of Warsaw and loved the peculiarities of its language, and that they felt disconnected from Israel and the Holocaust. All agreed, though, that they wanted to be both Polish and Jewish and were searching for ways to feel fully connected to both identities. They also knew that a commitment to Judaism would lead to unforeseen challenges. One woman revealed that her son had started to wear a skullcap. She worried that this put him in danger and wished that he would wear the skullcap only at home. This led to a broader discussion about leading a double life.

One man spoke about the difficulty of wanting to tell his wife and children that he was Jewish but being unable to do so. He said he would like to be able to "wear his Jewishness" more easily. On one occasion, he was "caught" standing on the fringes of a Jewish event by his brother-in-law, who asked him what he was doing there given he was not a Jew. Startled, he mumbled something that seemed to satisfy his brother-in-law. He said it didn't occur to him at the time to reply with the same question.

The group recalled that life was easier for them during Communist times. No one had money then, but there was time for a more active social life since everyone worked the same limited number of hours each day. Then, they felt connected. Now, they said, they only felt isolation. I wondered if this idealization of their past lives had a deeper meaning. Perhaps the rigidity and repression of communism on some level represented the "burying of secrets," while democracy represented the freedom to "know." Just as they wished to return to those simpler times, so too, perhaps, they wished to return to a time when they did not know.

In the middle of one session, someone suddenly began banging violently on the walls outside the meeting room. The group leader, sitting with her back to the window, had forgotten to lower the blinds. With her heart racing, she approached the window and lowered the blinds without investigating the disturbance. Everyone in the room seemed uncomfortable and a sense of danger lingered, lacing through the trivial chatter in the room. The group leader felt paralyzed and unable to open a discussion about the disturbance. Later, in supervision, she told me, "I should have discussed it, because it was happening to everyone at that moment, but couldn't because I was paralyzed within." She felt threatened and vulnerable. Her individuality and professional identity were lost in that moment. She said the only thing that crossed her mind was that "they shoot Jews."

At the next session, when a member wanted to discuss anti-Semitism, the leader took the opportunity to ask about people's responses to the disturbance the prior week. One woman said that she had felt an intense level of anxiety that she thinks will never go away. Her mother had run away from dangerous situations several times during the war and always feared being shot. Another member's mother swam across the Vista river with pictures of her family under her hat, and was caught and almost shot by the Russians. One member wondered whether the guards would protect them.

This led to a discussion of doors and windows. Windows were always closed in their homes. Most, however, preferred to have doors open, including the woman who had not yet told her daughter about being Jewish. She complained that although she liked the doors in her house to remain open, her husband liked doors closed. I wondered if any of the members considered the deeper meaning of this phenomenon. Perhaps open doors represented an ability to make a quick getaway.

Many members were particularly interested in determining how to best integrate the two religions into their lives. Most members continued to pray using the prayers they had learned as children. But they wondered whether they should bury dead parents who had Jewish roots according to the Catholic tradition or Jewish tradition. One revealed her mother told her she was Jewish on her deathbed but made her promise to have a church wedding.

Another woman said that she realized that the same kind of split happened within herself. She considered herself a Jew but was not always interested in Jewish issues. There were moments when she wished she didn't have to make a choice between Judaism and Catholicism. She spoke of her inner sadness about no longer feeling grounded in any religion. One man said that he associated sadness with being Jewish, but otherwise did not feel Jewish. He had not decided what to tell his children.

Another woman said she felt Jewish when she read about Jewish traditions but could neither bring herself to incorporate the religion into her daily life nor attend synagogue. Someone else said that he didn't know what it felt like to be a Jew, but that he felt

Jewish whenever he heard anti-Semitic rhetoric. Another member felt very connected to Judaism and its traditions, but had yet to tell anyone outside the group that she was Jewish.

At one meeting, a woman who had decided to leave the group with the idea that she was going to continue to live her life as a Catholic—and keep her roots secret—called to say that she had had a change of heart. She had been standing in front of a mirror, and with her husband in the room, she heard herself blurt out that she was a Jew. He said that he had thought so. She didn't ask him how he had known, and he didn't say. She wanted him to be curious and ask, but there was only an uncomfortable silence. She had also wanted to be more curious herself, but found herself unable to ask her mother. She thought of her heritage while visiting the cemetery where her grandmother was buried, thinking of it as a Jewish cemetery . . . but, in fact, it was Catholic.

Most group members, like this woman, struggled with their "two sides." They were both a part of the comfortable majority—and a hated minority.

11 The Work Revisited: Two Years Later

Two years passed and pieces of the puzzle still awaited completion. I wondered how the rise of anti-Semitism in Europe and the Middle East was affecting the development of new and struggling Jewish identities in Poland.

I had kept in touch with several individuals, including the staff member Magda, who had asked for my help in lighting Sabbath candles at the camp meeting in Rychwald. She had since made the decision to transfer her children to the Ronald S. Lauder School. Magda's husband was supportive of her choice, while her mother was strongly against it. The school was well run, offered a well-rounded education, and even accepted children with no Jewish roots.

Magda wrote me a letter with news regarding a significant development in her life. She had coaxed her mother to see her grandchildren in a school play. Against her better judgment and fearful about being in this school with "Jews," her mother agreed to go. Nearing the end of the performance, the children sang a song that was clearly a "Jewish" song. Magda was totally taken by surprise when she heard her mother sing along under her breath and saw tears running down her face. Tears welled up in Magda as well, for it confirmed what she had long suspected, that she was Jewish. At that moment, she felt that she had made the right decision regarding her children's education. She wanted them to feel whole and sure about their identity, as she had not.

Later, her mother told her that at the start of the war, her parents had saved her from the death camps by sending her to England on the "kinder transport." The song that her grandchildren sang that day was the very song that she and the other children on the transport sang on the journey to feel closer to home and their parents. The kinder transport was a short accommodation made by the Germans to allow children to be transported to England. Many of those children saved never saw their parents again.

Some time after I received that letter, I called Magda to say hello and to get an opinion about when might be a good time to return for follow-up interviews. Magda informed me that she had heard that several members of the work groups had left Poland in order to follow their Judaism in a more open environment. Others, like herself, remained, following their Jewish roots in Poland. With a smile in her voice, she suggested a date for my return. The date was of particular significance to her. It would be the day of her daughter's Bat-Mitzvah. She added that she would feel honored if I would come and witness the first of her children bringing Jewish tradition back to her family. I accepted the invitation with honor.

Boarding the flight felt familiar. It was like going to see an old friend in order to "catch up." I hoped to be seeing familiar faces and looked forward to hearing their stories. An old friend and former assistant to Rabbi Schudrich met me at the airport. On the ride into town he briefed me on the status of people that I had known. The ride from the airport was much longer than I remembered. Owning a vehicle had become much easier. This added to the congestion of old roads unable to accommodate the new rhythm of the city. Democratization was in full swing. The trip that had previously taken no more than fifteen minutes now took closer to an hour.

The city's architecture told its history. Prewar buildings with their charming detail stood next to the barren utilitarian structures of the Communist era, as modern office buildings—symbols of capitalism—loomed over both, intermittently poking through the skyline. Soon, the old city and my hotel were in view. I was not in touch with the pulse of the city as I had been when I leased and stayed in an apartment. However, I had chosen a hotel that was near to my "old neighborhood." In this way, I could revisit the merchants and streets that had been a second home to me. I quickly settled in and started to schedule interviews. And I soon discovered who had left Poland and who had stayed.

Tadeusz, who had long wanted to "cut the bouquet" of his budding Judaism, had immigrated with his wife to Canada. Tanya had sent both of her children to Israel to study and to feel proud about their heritage. The children subsequently chose to remain in Israel although they enjoyed visiting their mother in Poland. She planned to join them in Israel as soon as it became possible. Rysia, the young girl who had been told that she should be thrown "to the gas" because she had Israeli flags in her room, was studying at a university in Milan, Italy. There, she met many other young Jews at temple, which she visited frequently. She said that being Jewish in Italy "felt comfortable and normal." Ula, the young woman who felt that her biological clock was ticking and was not sure that she would find a suitable husband in Poland, was now in Israel.

Regina, the woman who had been peeling potatoes with her mother when she discovered, had spent a year studying in Jerusalem. Although very committed to Jewish life, she felt the need to find more flexibility in Orthodox Judaism. Her fiance, Tomasz, who had stayed in Poland when she made the decision to study in Israel, married and moved to Australia. Regina said she missed him and was sorry that her decision to explore Judaism in Israel meant losing the man with whom she wanted to spend a lifetime.

I learned that Tomasz, while waiting for Regina to return, had made the decision that orthodoxy was not for him. He had no desire to follow her to Israel. Rather, he had a great desire to travel and see Jewish life in countries that interested him, such as the

United States and Australia. He was not sure how realistic this was or how possible it would be to achieve his goals, but he told Michael of his dreams. Michael offered him the opportunity to go to New York for a few days with a group of students. Tomasz jumped at the chance.

His first morning in the United States, Tomasz called me and asked whether we could meet for coffee at the top of the Empire State building, saying it would be the easiest place for him to find. I was happy to meet him. When I saw him, he was taking in New York with eyes and head spinning 360 degrees. I caught him and said hello. He said "hi" and we both laughed. We had a cup of coffee and drove to the Village for sightseeing and gift shopping. Tomasz had the address of a store that sold games and books he wanted to take home. He also wanted to see several synagogues in New York so that he could understand the religion in a different context. He was saddened about his breakup with Regina, but felt that their respective levels of commitment to Judaism were very different. His interests were in ethnicity and tradition, while she gravitated toward religious studies.

Soon after his return to Poland, he applied to go to Sydney, Australia. In doing so, he met a young woman who also wanted to explore Australia and the possibilities of Jewish life. They began spending time together and eventually decided to go on their journey as a married couple. The decision to marry and leave Poland happened very quickly.

Jacek, the homeopathic doctor, moved to Germany with his wife and son. While in Poland, he was circumcised and converted to Judaism. Though his wife was not willing to convert, Jacek wanted to expose his son to Judaism and the Jewish tradition. When old enough, his son would be in a position to decide which religion he would follow. Jacek did not think that pursuing Judaism in Germany could be any more difficult than it was in Poland.

Felix, who had connections to his Jewish roots through the Jewish music cassettes of his grandmother, was still in Warsaw continuing his architecture studies. He spent time with a Jewish couple around Jewish holidays and celebrated with them, though he said he was not religious himself. When we met for coffee, he showed me the two "talismans" he carries with him everywhere he goes: an umbrella given to him by his beloved grandmother and a kipa. He said that they both covered his head and protected him.

The following morning was Saturday, the day of the Bat-Mitzvah. I walked the twenty minutes from the old city to the only temple in Warsaw. The approach to the temple appeared more guarded than I had remembered. This was understandable. Months earlier, a home made bomb had been thrown through a window, causing some fire damage.

It was a very hot day, but the windows of the temple were only partially open. I opened the door and several young boys rushed past me playfully. Inside, life was teeming. There were approximately 150 people in attendance. Magda's daughter read her portion of the Torah brilliantly. Magda had also wanted to read one or two sentences, and did so. At the end of morning prayers, Magda's daughter stood on the podium and gave her speech. In it, she described her happiness at being a Jew. Her mother added that she was proud of her daughter's determination, adding that the Bat-Mitzvah had been her daughter's idea. After the ceremony, I spoke to Magda and her daughter. Magda was pleased, although somewhat worried about the unknown future of Jews in Poland. Her daughter, meanwhile, did not seem conflicted with her choice.

I remembered a visit I had made to the Ronald S. Lauder School a few years earlier. All the children were baking challahs to bring home. They seemed totally delighted with the project. The director of the school told me that she did not know how many parents were Jewish, but knew that many or most of them did not have the background or knowledge to educate their children in Jewish traditions. In effect, it was the children who would be teaching their parents about the culture of Judaism. The children were without conflict and, with parental support, could easily absorb the material they learned at school.

Since a few years had passed, I went to visit the school again. I wanted to see how information about Jewish culture was affecting the students' lives outside of school. One boy had learned quickly to remove his kipa when outside of his home or school. One day, while being walked by his father to a friend's home for a play date, the two were verbally accosted by youths who yelled "Jews to the gas." Although holding his father's hand, he was frightened. It was difficult for his father to explain to him why the boys were yelling at them. He told him not to wear his kipa in the street in the future. The incident troubled the boy. He couldn't understand why the youths didn't like Jews, since there were kids in his school that were not Jews but were nice to him. Nevertheless, he had learned the "rules of engagement."

A young girl noticed that girls outside of her school wore beautiful white dresses for their church confirmation. She asked her mother why she needed to be different than most of her friends. Her mother explained that the dress was part of a Catholic ritual and that they, as Jews, had different rituals. She told her daughter, however, that they would go shopping for a beautiful pink dress. These parents addressed the sensitivities of their children in a way that perhaps softened the differences, helping them to better integrate their new-found identity.

Commitment to Broken Chain remained as well. Even though outside funding had run out, members of the group continued to gather together each week, always at the same time. The group had formed a "grass roots" network. I received a call inviting me to see a video of a Broken Chain meeting. They wanted me to see the continuation of the work that I had begun. An Israeli film director who I had helped while she was filming in Poland had privately taped a session for them. The viewing was a gift. I cherished every face, every word, and every moment.

On my last day in Warsaw, I received a call from a man named Piotr who wanted me to hear his story. This happened often during my stays in Poland. I told him I would be more than happy to speak with him. We met early that evening. An elegant man in his thirties, Piotr told me with a smile on his face that he was proud of his story and wanted me to know that being Jewish in Poland was becoming more acceptable.

His story started with a planned vacation. After having been married for a year, he decided to visit his uncle in Israel. The visit coincided with the assassination of Yitzhak Rabin. Piotr recalled that everyone was in mourning. He remembers seeing candles lit on every street and sitting with his uncle over drinks at a hotel in Jerusalem. As they spoke about the future of Jews in Israel, it became apparent to him that his uncle considered himself to be Jewish. This surprised Piotr. He knew that his uncle had been very active in the underground during World War II and that he had escaped capture by leaving Poland. He also knew that he had met a Jewish woman in Europe and had followed her to Palestine. Piotr asked his uncle whether he was Jewish by conversion. His uncle smiled, saying he had no need to convert: he had always been Jewish.

Piotr was shocked that he had not been told, particularly since his wife was a Catholic woman from a deeply religious family. Upon his return to Poland, he confronted his father. His father told him that he had thought life would be easier for Piotr if he didn't know. Piotr said that he suddenly felt like he didn't know who he was. The rug had been pulled out from under him. He gave it a lot of thought but couldn't come to terms with his new religious identity. It felt very complicated, so he didn't focus on it.

Months later, he saw an advertisement for the Jewish hotline in the local paper. He clipped the ad and kept it for several months before calling. Finally, he called and was told that he could come to explore his Jewish roots on any level that he was comfortable with. He started by going to Rabbi Schudrich's Friday evening lectures once or twice a month. Slowly, he began to go weekly and even started going to synagogue on Friday evening. He said he heard melodies that touched his heart and made it beat. During this time, his wife became a witness to his journey. Piotr started going to synagogue on Saturdays and began taking more frequent trips to Israel. He was beginning to think more about Jewish life and was attracted to modern orthodoxy.

At work, he took leave on religious holy days and started working longer hours during the week so that he could avoid coming to work on the Sabbath. One of his coworkers started to say negative things about his work schedule to a new director. He said he knew he had to respond to the charges, so he told his director that he was Jewish and needed to leave early on Fridays, but that he would be willing to make up the time during the week. The director understood, telling him not to worry as he was Jewish, too. Piotr saw this as a stroke of luck and felt more secure at work. Around this time, his wife became pregnant and she approached him about converting to Judaism. She said that since they were going to have a child, it was important for her that they follow the same religious path together. Piotr had reservations, but she convinced him that she had thought through it seriously. They told her parents of their decision: her mother cried and her father warned of dangers. Today, Piotr's wife keeps a kosher home, but they compromise when going to her parents' home for dinner. Piotr wanted me to know that he and his wife feel good about the future of Jewish families in Poland.

I listened to his and all the stories I heard with great interest. Had Poland changed for the better in the previous two years? For an answer, I decided to speak with the one person who actively kept the pulse of the Jewish community in Poland, Rabbi Michael Schudrich.

12 A Dialogue with the Rabbi of Poland

Rabbi Michael Schudrich is creating a safe haven in Poland for those curious about their Jewish roots. I called him during one of his many visits to New York and asked to speak with him about Jewish identity in Poland today. He happily agreed to meet with me. I present his thoughts here in his own words.

Vera Muller-Paisner: When did you first go to Poland?

Rabbi Michael Schudrich: The first time I went to Poland was in 1973. I had just graduated from high school, and that was my first encounter. I then went back to Poland several times in the seventies to see what I could find out. In 1979, I began meeting people roughly our age . . . meaning of the postwar generation, and realized that there were still young Jews in Poland.

I started to work in Poland in March of 1990 for the Ronald S. Lauder Foundation. I moved there in the fall of 1992 and lived there until the fall of 1998. I returned in the spring of 2000 as Rabbi of Warsaw . . . and then also later as Rabbi of Lodz.

Are people continuing to discover Jewish roots there?

People are still discovering, but there are two levels of discovery. One is the moment that you find out. The other is the moment that you decide to do something about it. Neither are necessarily clear-cut moments.

There are people who will say: I remember from the time that I was fifteen, I thought that something didn't make sense in the family. When I was twenty-seven I kind of was pretty sure, but only at forty-eight did I find out! Or there are people that . . . a guy came into my office about a year ago looking about sixty. He told me that his mother was eighty-nine and eight days before he came to see me, his mother had told him for the first time that she was Jewish. He didn't have a clue. Everything had made sense in his life, and he had no idea. So there is the moment of discovery and then there is the moment when people decide to come forward.

I distinctly remember one young woman from Lublin. She had discovered three years before she came to see me that her maternal grandparents were really named Moishe Fine and Chaya Lamberger. She was about twenty-three at the time and married for three years with two little kids. It took her three years and tremendous encouragement from her husband to come and see me to find out what she is supposed to do about it.

Was her husband Jewish?

No. As a matter of fact her husband later converted to Judaism. His story was that his family was also from Lublin and his grandfather had hidden a Jew who escaped from the death camp Majdanek. Before the end of the war, someone had informed on him, and both the Jew and his grandfather were murdered by the Nazis. The son somehow felt compelled to finish the work of his grandfather. In other words, his grandfather had set out to save a Jewish life, so he was going to become that Jew.

Do you think that discovering that you are a Jew in Poland is more difficult to deal with than a similar discovery made elsewhere, such as someone discovering that they are adopted?

There may be more in common than not with the rest of the world. When people discover that they are adopted, I assume there's a spectrum of reactions. There are those that say, well, I always figured that I was not really their kid because I'm short with black curly hair and my parents are tall, skinny, and blond. Then there are those that are shocked, deny it, and don't want to know, or want to know and are fascinated by it. Frankly, I think there is far more in common with the discovery of other secrets than not.

But what about the broader social and political environment? If you find out the secret of being Jewish or adopted and you live in New Jersey or New York, then it is largely an internal issue. But if you find out that you are a Jew in Poland, doesn't it affect you and your family socially?

Perhaps the greatest problem is that nobody knows. It's unclear how the rest of the world will react. It's unclear how your family will react. It's unclear how your friends will react. So there is a tremendous feeling of lack of security and thinking that I don't know what's going to happen. To a human being that is just about the worst thing that could be. It's a complete lack of security.

Is it because anti-Semitism is rampant in Poland?

No. Anti-Semitism is not rampant in Poland. It exists in Poland as it exists throughout the Christian world, and the Muslim world. It's this fear of not knowing what is going to happen. One has to realize that Poland before the war was really a multiethnic religious community and country. The war created a perceived monoethnicity of one religion: everybody is Catholic, everybody is Polish. The Ukrainian minority, the German minority, the Belarussian minority, the Roman minority, and the Jewish minority were either murdered or expelled, and forgotten about. In order to really be Polish today, it is perceived not by all, but by some, that you need to be Catholic. So if you're Jewish you're saying two things. First, you're saying that you're not Catholic, and then, you're also Jewish. It is hard to say which is more important. You can compare it to several thousand Poles who after 1989 discovered that they are really German. Some of them are having problems because they no longer feel that they are true Poles.

Sounds as if nationalism is highly important in Poland.

Americans have a hard time conceptualizing this idea. National identity is very important throughout Europe. We Americans perceive that as being antitolerant. Europeans would consider that just normal.

However, the census of 1921 in Poland encouraged Jews to claim Judaism as a nationality. You could either be a Pole or Jew but not both.

So what? Does that make it anti-Semitic?

I didn't say that it was anti-Semitic. If you had to make a choice to either live as a Pole or live as a Jew, if you chose to live as a Pole, you would not be considered to be part of the Jewish community and would not be in a position to get help from the community should you need it.

The concept of hyphenated identity is American. It probably did not exist in America in 1921 either. We're talking about a post-World War II concept of the melting pot and ask why the Poles did not do it in 1921. I don't think the Americans did it in 1921. You're very right that before the war people would identify themselves either as Jews or Poles. It was important how you would define yourself. I think it continues to be very important to differentiate.

When persons discover that they are Jewish in Poland today, is there a place for them to be a Pole-Jew or Jew-Pole? In other words, can we use two nouns, not an adjective and a noun? Of course, when we say "American Jew," we mean an American and a Jew. Most American Jews feel completely at home in their Judaism, however they express it, as well as clearly at home with being an American. It's so melted together in the United States that the hyphen has disappeared. The hyphen has melted away. Is that possible in Poland today?

The reality is that when a person at the age of fifteen, twenty-seven, thirty-eight, or forty-nine discovers that he or she is Jewish, we often fail to be sensitive to the reality that they were someone before; they had an identity before. It's not that a person who discovers at thirty-seven that his mother is Jewish was hibernating his entire life. He was something, someone, for thirty-seven years. Whatever it was, it was an identity. Whether it was a Polish atheist, a Polish Catholic, or a Polish Communist, he was Polish. Therefore, that is his ethnic cultural point of departure. Where does Judaism play into that identity? Can he become a Polish Jew?

Why would anyone want to be a Jew at all?

That's a separate issue. For now, let's say that although the idea of Judaism may be fascinating, the fact is that he or she is Polish. Not that they want to be, they are! Culturally and ethnically they are Polish. So what do they do now with this new religious ethnic identity?

Part of the success with American Jewish hyphenated identity is that we have grown up with it. We grew up with the Fourth of July and Rosh Hashanah hand in hand. I think when a person grows up with this idea, it evolves naturally for that person.

It would be interesting to compare this to the people that grew up with white and black parents in the 1970s. How did they express their ethnic and their color identity? At least those people struggled with it their entire lives since there was no hiding it. People here discover at sixteen or twenty-five that they have a different or second identity. Some have opted to say that they have a different identity while others say they have an additional identity.

There is something fundamentally unnatural in trying to place that second identity on someone after early childhood. The fascination is whether this is a new identity or a second identity. I have not found a difference between those who have decided to have a more traditional expression of Judaism, those whom we would call religious, and those who are not. I find that some of the most religious young Jewish people I know are also fiercely Polish. They are very proud to be living in Poland and feel very tied to Polish culture. We are not dealing with huge numbers, though, so it is hard to plot exactly.

How many numbers are we talking about?

Thousands, several thousands, if not more. I am referring to those who have opted to come in contact with me. There are those who have not come in contact with me. Within that group, you have those who maybe read about what is happening in the Jewish community because it touches them and they feel connected, but don't come. Then there are those who don't want to hear about it, and those who simply don't care. I'm not sure which in the second two groups is closer to becoming Jewish. I think I know which one it is.

Which one would you guess?

The ones who absolutely don't want to know about it. I remember you said that it took thirteen weeks for people to respond to ads placed in major newspapers when you started your groups in Poland. Well, sometimes it takes thirteen years. It's very difficult for people to try to place a new, additional, or replacement identity on top of a preexisting identity. I think that is the biggest problem. The fact that it is taking place in Poland, where people perceive that there is some anti-Semitism, doesn't help. I think that it is a struggle regardless of where it takes place. The fundamental struggle is not place specific; it is specific to the individual.

I remember speaking to several people in the mid-1990s who were afraid to pursue their Judaism because they feared that they or their parents would lose their jobs. Was this the reality?

Yes. People were afraid that they would lose their jobs, but you know what the problem is? Poles really don't like it when you don't tell them the truth the first time. In other words, if you're a Jew, tell me. Don't tell me that you're not a Jew, and then twenty years later say that you are. A Pole doesn't want you to celebrate Christmas with him and then find out that you're Jewish. It's not honest.

But what if they didn't know, if they hadn't yet discovered when they were celebrating Christmas?

A lot of people didn't know, but the thought is that maybe they should have known. Sometimes when they say that "she doesn't know that she's Jewish," what they mean is that she's the only one in town who doesn't know.

Is it really dangerous to say that you're Jewish in Poland today? Part of it is that Poles don't like people switching in the middle. If you were Polish yesterday and are Jewish today, it may look like some kind of deception. Poles tend to have very intense relationships. The postwar generation didn't know, so now that they know, they are telling them. It's a little weird, but nevertheless it's being done. The older generation, however, the parents, they knew and didn't tell. Some of their friends are going to resent them for it. Plus, some people are anti-Semitic.

The point is also that in America, it's not that we don't have anti-Semites in America, but a Jew doesn't need to try and become good friends with an anti-Semite. A Jew may need to eliminate befriending about 20 percent of the population. Maybe the same 20 percent as in Poland, but in Poland, when a Jew is hiding his Jewish identity, he could easily become friends with someone who is anti-Semitic and not know it. That's where it gets complicated.

Has there been a decrease in anti-Semitism since 1989?

What is my hesitation? I think it's that Jews are becoming less relevant. Who cares? More people are focused today on the car or computer or CD player than they are about if you're a Jew or German. Is that good or bad? It's both.

Do you think that choices and freedom have made it less relevant?

I'd like to believe that things are getting more normal. Is it true? I'm not sure how abnormal it was to begin with. I think a lot of this fear was self-imagined, but just because it's self-perceived doesn't mean that there are no anti-Semites. The Jews' perception of anti-Semitism may have excluded contact with each other in many places in the world.

What about the people who are anti-Semitic and discover that they have Jewish roots? Do you come into contact with them at all?

Yes. I do come in contact with people who had been anti-Semitic before discovery.

What happens to those who experience having an enemy within?

Let me tell you a story. We have a young couple who fell in love in high school and got married soon after graduation. She then discovered that she had Jewish roots. She became somewhat interested in this discovery, but for the first three years she didn't care

much. After that she decided that she wanted to make Sabbath dinner. The husband's parents got all upset, saying, "You can't do this!"
The more they said no, the more the husband supported the wife.
After several months, the parents finally admitted that the reason
that they were so much against it is because they are Jewish!

So we see that he's Jewish, she's Jewish, and the kicker is that
they were both skinheads in high school! They have actually
become traditional and observant. She keeps Sabbath, covers her
hair, and he puts on Tefilin. He says that sometimes he looks at
himself in the mirror and can't believe that it's him. He still doesn't
want to be on television because of his parents. His parents aren't
so comfortable with it, and he has a twin brother who also feels
uncomfortable with exposure and does not identify with being
Jewish. His twin is not a skin head. They see each other but his
Jewish identity is not forthcoming.

To answer the question why people do it, I think it is for the
spark of the Jewish soul. I want for someone to disprove that this is
not the reason. Not to say it in secular terms, for many people I
think that it is a deeply spiritual experience. They must be experiencing a lack of satisfaction with their spirituality at that time, and
when they realize their lack of connection to something spiritual,
they actually feel the need to do something about it, because of the
realization they are not what they think they are. It becomes very
redemptive for them. It plays an important role and things begin to
make sense.

So why look for Jewish roots in the midst of anti-Semitism? No
one is looking for Jewish roots. They have Jewish roots. Plus, there
are people who are looking because they feel a connection.

*There are also those who discover that they are Jews and turn in the
other direction. We don't hear from them.*

Yes. We see the ones who think that they are Jewish and start to
look. Among those, there are two basic groups. One is people who

are really Jewish but don't have any proof, and their Jewish identity has been passed to them in a nonverbal form, through value systems or family structure. The second group is alienated from the mainstream. Since they are so alienated, they seek solace by saying in fact that they are minorities. We have a handful of those people also. When it becomes clear that this is their situation, it generally becomes painful because they realize that they are different and perhaps disturbed. There is one older woman, for example, who has become convinced that she is Jewish. She is in her sixties. She is disheveled, unkempt. People around her have been calling her "kike" as an insult. So she began to believe that she is a "kike."

But interestingly, as time goes on, people are starting to bring in their siblings, their parents, their first cousins.

It is interesting to see how people need to be able to relate to an identity, to a group, as does this woman who is alienated. Either they need to be alienated and be different, as part of a minority, or they have a need to be part of a group that's a minority. It is a form of identity.

If you're not going to be part of the majority then you may as well be part of a minority. Otherwise you're nobody.

Does the connection to a discovered authentic past solidify an authentic future? As a rabbi, what is your vision for Jewish life in Poland?

I don't have a vision. It is theirs to create. My vision for my work is to create a welcoming environment for people to encounter and experience Jewish tradition in life. What they do with it has to be their choice. People who have gone through an intense experience of discovering that they are Jewish later in life need to be given the space to make the decision of what they want to do.

How are people tolerating the difference between who they thought they were, and who they really are?

They are who they always were. The question is who they are in addition to who they were.

Yes, and how they are going to integrate the two.

Right. I'm not a big fan of advocating that they have to leave "X" in order to become "Y."

What if they truly feel Catholic and religious. What do they do then?

Ahah! They can remain religious.

And remain Catholic?

And Jewish. They have to find their own way. It's very important to be patient. I'm not going through what they are going through.

How do these people see you? What do they expect of you? How do they see your role in reference to their life?

Why is that important?

Because you're the one helping them to find their spirituality.

I think I help to create a safe space for their exploration. If I am creating a safe space, it is important for people to know that the safe space is accessible when they need it. I am helping them to understand that there is a place for them in Judaism.

13 Understanding Family History

As members of a family, we experience the world both internally and externally. Our personal narrative interweaves familial dynamics and legacies within historical and cultural contexts. This all interfaces with society's perception of who we are. In essence, we recognize ourselves and are reflected in the eyes of others. Changes in any of these internal and external dimensions must be constantly integrated to maintain a coherent sense of self. As we age, therefore, we evolve and negotiate multiple identities. Personal identity is never fixed. Boundaries remain fluid and open, though the individual core remains intact as it links to the larger group collective.[11]

As part of one's identity, nationality and religion are not usually considered to be substitutes for each another. Poles who have recently discovered their Jewish roots understandably do not want to relinquish their identity as Poles, even if they choose to embrace their Jewish legacy.[12] In Poland today, families of victims and families of perpetrators are now in the position of being able to reconcile their own specific family narrative with historical reality. Just as children of victims struggle to cope with revelations about their family's past, so too are children of perpetrators struggling to overcome years of Communist propaganda that led Poles to believe that they were heroic victims of Nazi atrocities and never collaborators. For example, only in 2001 did Poland's president beg forgiveness for the wartime massacre of 1,600 Jewish villagers, who sixty years earlier were burned alive in a barn by their Polish neighbors in a town called Jedwabne.

This desire to want to know and to take responsibility for the past represents the beginning of healing. But those who "discover" will need time to integrate their new identity into their own personal narrative. The restoration of a family's true narrative offers a sense of wholeness but demands tenacity. There is a universal fear that giving up one identity for another will mean a loss of security. It takes courage and determination to push through the ambivalence of integrating one's new identity into one's old sense of self. But it must be done to feel whole again and to heal.

Poland itself is a good example of the struggle between wanting to explore a newly discovered identity and wanting to remain externally secure and the same. Absorbing and integrating new-found knowledge into one's own personal narrative may help one better accept differences in others—and thus may give hope for the future.

Notes

Introduction

1. E.J. Kessler, "Gen. Clark's Next War: Conquer the Democrats?" *Forward*, January 31, 2003.
2. James Harding, "The Complicated Candidate," *Financial Times*, July 31, 2004.
3. K. Gebert, "Jewish identities in Poland: New, old and imaginary," in J. Webber, ed., *Jewish identities in New Europe* (London: Littman Library of Jewish Civilization, 1994), 161–167.
4. Personal communication with Rabbi Michael Schudrich.

1

5. Polyglot analysis (multilingual) with Herbert Holt. He spoke most of the languages that I dreamt in, including French and German.

2

6. Dori Laub and N.C. Auerhahn, "Knowing and not knowing massive psychic trauma: Forms of traumatic memory," *International Journal of Psychoanalysis* 3 (1993): 287-302.
7. Personal communication with Maria Orwid of the Department of Child and Adolescent Psychiatry at Jagellonian Collegium Medicum, Krakow, Poland. Similar outcomes were found in small sample studies in Poland.

3

8. 6 Twarda Street is the main address of the Ronald S. Lauder
Foundation in Poland. It is adjacent to the Nozyk Synagogue.
9. American Jewish Committee, *The Jewish Communities of Nazi-
Occupied Europe* (New York: Howard Fertig, 1982).

6

10. More than three hundred crosses planted outside the Auschwitz
concentration camp were later removed and taken to a Franciscan
monastery.

13

11. Erik H. Erikson, *Identity and the Life Cycle* (New York: W.W.
Norton & Company, 1959), 18–19.
12 K. Gebert, "Jewish identities in Poland: New, old and imaginary,"
in J. Webber, ed., *Jewish Identities in New Europe* (London: Littman
Library of Jewish Civilization, 1994), 161–167.